Behind Closed Doors

JENNY TOMLIN

Behind Closed Doors

*A true story of abuse, neglect
and survival against the odds*

HODDER

Copyright © 2005 by Jenny Tomlin

First published in Great Britain in 2005
by Hodder and Stoughton
A division of Hodder Headline

This paperback edition published in 2006
This edition published 2008 for Index Books Ltd

The right of Jenny Tomlin to be identified as the Author
of the Work has been asserted by her in accordance with
the Copyright, Designs and Patents Act 1988.

A Hodder paperback

1

Names have been changed to protect the identity of individuals.

A CIP catalogue record for this title is available from the British Library

ISBN 978-0-340-92520-1

Typeset in Sabon by Hewer Text Ltd, Edinburgh
Printed and bound in Great Britain by Clays Ltd, St Ives plc

Hodder Headline's policy is to use papers that are natural, renewable and
recyclable products and made from wood grown in sustainable forests.
The logging and manufacturing processes are expected to conform to the
environmental regulations of the country of origin.

Hodder and Stoughton Ltd
A division of Hodder Headline
338 Euston Road
London NW1 3BH

Photographs are from the author's collection except the following:
The Hackney Archives Department, London Borough of Hackney, pages 3
top, 4 bottom, 5 bottom (donated by H. Law, 1974)

This book is dedicated
to the memory of Auntie

Contents

Acknowledgements

My sincere love and gratitude go out to the following.

To Martine, my daughter, my friend and one of the most beautiful people I know. I am privileged to have you in my life and thank you for all your support. Your belief in me has never wavered and I love you unconditionally.

To Kim, my wonderful sister, carer and adviser. You allowed me to open memories, and without you this book would not have been written. Thanks for the laughter.

To LJ, my beautiful young son: I watch you grow with pride. Mum and dad John love you very much.

To Alan, the love of my life, and my rock when things were difficult. An amazing husband and friend.

To Carrine, Howard and Lewis Batty: love you. To Jaine Brent, my friend and agent. Your belief in my book and your determination to get it published were remarkable. I love you dearly. Thanks for the nightly chats.

Acknowledgements

To all the team at Hodder and Stoughton, my wonderful publishers. Thanks for the opportunity to tell my story. To my lawyer Rhian Williams at Clinton's, for sorting out the legal stuff and keeping me safe, and to Laura Holman, a great accountant.

To wonderful friends, especially Antony Read: you are a lovely man and always there.

To Sylvia Wales and family, Sherri Jeffrey and Miriam Ridsdale. To Gina and Brian Parker and Ian Palmer (Little Ian).

To Barry and John in Spain, for teaching me to forgive and move on. Thanks also to the lovely Russell Grant!

To Karen and George and Kerry and all the gang in Hornchurch. To the adorable Norma Heyman. To Eydie and Steve . . . up North! And to John Falconer: hope you are happy.

To all those who have been in my life, good or bad. I thank you. Why? Because through life's experiences we become who we are, and you all made this book possible.

My final thoughts must go to Chris, my younger brother and the beautiful man who touched our lives for such a short time. And of course to Auntie, forever with me. I love you both.

Introduction

It is never easy to dig deep into painful buried memories. But after the death of my father I found I needed to put events of the past down in writing to escape the hold they had over me. This book is the result. Writing it proved to be a fascinating, eventful, roller-coaster ride. I laughed, cried, remembered people and places I had forgotten, rediscovered friends and learned so much about myself, who I was and who I have become. My intention was not to hurt anyone, dead or still living, but rather to tell my story truthfully – the good, the bad and the ugly faces of a childhood which was immensely tough but which ultimately made me very strong.

My early years were empty of all the things we take for granted today. There were no Christmas or birthday presents – at least, none that were not snatched away to be immediately resold. There was little food, and no love, warmth or cleanliness – only violence, abuse, greed, lust, loneliness and filth. As a child, I felt that no adult was ever interested in what I had to say. I was ignored, dismissed and pushed away, even by those in authority whose job it was to help and protect children. Many times I tried to get one of those adults to listen and help me. None ever did.

Today much has improved. Child protection services are better, and children are listened to and respected far more. But still many young people slip through the net. There are children out there who are suffering just as I did and who feel just as alone, ignored and unloved because an adult who could help them is not listening. It is our job, every one of us, to find those children, listen to them and help them. As I wrote down my own childhood experiences I thought of the many others who have gone through similar anguish and fear, and of those who are still doing so even now. I hope that anyone who has suffered in the same way will realise, after reading this book, that they are not alone.

What I went through made me determined to give my own children what I never had: to bring them up surrounded by safety, warmth and love; to listen to them, respect them and help them feel valued. These things are the right of every child. This book is for all those children who are suffering in silence, loneliness and fear. And for all those who knew me and who remember the little girl with the dirty face and no shoes who tried so hard to belong. This is the story that no one ever saw. The story of what went on behind closed doors.

I

Cherbury Street

My first memories are of waking to the dull thud of my mother being thrown against the wall in the next room, and to the sound of my father's voice raging at her. As I listened to the thumps, whimpers and roars just a few feet away I lay in my bed silent and terrified, curled into a ball with the covers pulled high to try to block it all out.

Through the thin wall my father hurled abuse at my mother. 'Yer fucking cow, yer useless mare, think yer can say no, do yer? I'm yer husband and I've got my rights! Now get on this bed and give me what I want or yer'll get some more of this.' Another thud, followed by a shriek and whimpers of pain from my mother. A moment later her thin voice would be raised: 'Yer bastard, yer fucking bastard.' Another thump, another shriek. 'What did yer call me? I've got two parents, yer stupid cow.'

Next to me my brother Laurence, at five a year older than me, was on his knees, his small shoulders shuddering, his head pushed into the pillow to try to muffle the awful sounds. Across the room our baby sister Kim was crying in her cot. She was two, too young to understand what she was hearing, but old enough to know it was frightening and bad.

This scene was the same every morning. It was the way we started our day, and to us it was normal. But that did not make it any easier. My stomach would be clenched in a knot and I would pray over and over again, my clammy little palms stuck together under the covers, for the shouting and hitting to stop. Sometimes Laurence could not stand it any more. He would run into our parents' bedroom shouting, 'Stop it! Stop it! Leave her alone! Get off her!' and throw himself at Dad in a desperate attempt to protect Mum. Dad would hiss, 'Fuck off, yer little cunt', pick my brother up in one hand and throw him out of the room. Laurence would crash on to the floor and crawl back into our room, badly bruised and sobbing with pain and fear.

The next sound we would hear through the wall would be the grunts and gasps of our parents having sex. Of course, at our age we were never sure what these noises meant. We knew it was something Dad did to Mum that Mum did not want, and we knew that when they did it there was a lot of panting and grunting. And we knew it must be horrible – but at least when they did it Dad stopped attacking Mum.

Once it was over Mum would emerge from the bedroom, tying her old, frayed dressing gown around her thin body and holding her broken glasses. She would go into the kitchen and busy herself filling the kettle, putting it on the small hob and making tea. We would listen until we heard her taking Dad his breakfast, and when she had gone back to the kitchen the three of us would follow her. Mum would be sitting on the old wooden chair at the small table, her dressing gown falling open. We could see the bruises and cuts on her body, and there was often blood on the corner of her mouth or oozing from a cut on her face. She would be trying to mend her broken glasses with Sellotape or sticking plaster, tears streaming down her face, her whole body trembling so much that she could not hold the glasses steady. We would go and stand close to her, anxiously putting out a hand to touch her arm or saying, 'Don't cry, Mum.' She would glance at the door in case Dad saw us and then brush us away, telling us to go and get dressed and muttering, 'You'd better get out the house before yer father gets up.'

We would pick our clothes up from the floor where they had fallen the night before. We slept in our vests and knickers – we did not take them off for weeks at a time – and the rest was just put back on over the top. We were too small to manage dressing ourselves properly, so everything was back

5

to front and buttons were not done up. Laurence and I would dress Kim as best we could before the three of us went back to the kitchen, hoping for some breakfast.

Like the rest of the flat, the kitchen was dirty and smelly. On an old worn-out tray on the Formica-topped table stood a battered brown teapot and a few chipped mugs. Apart from a packet of tea, a sugar bowl and a partly used bottle of milk, our larder was usually bare. The milk, left standing all night, would have formed a film over the top and be starting to go sour. The sugar bowl was often empty, and on those days Mum would pour in some hot water to soak up the bits that had congealed at the bottom. The only food would be a few stale crusts of bread, but most of these were saved for Dad's favourite breakfast dish. Mum would put the crusts in a bowl, sprinkle sugar over them as liberally as possible and pour on boiling milk. This was served to him in bed, with his usual cup of tea and cigarette. For us children, breakfast was usually a cup of weak tea. The milk had been watered down to make it last longer, so to help the flavour we would put in whatever sugar was still available. If we were lucky we would get a 'nobby', the knobbly end of the previous day's loaf, to share.

After breakfast Mum shooed us into the street to fend for ourselves and told us not to come back till teatime. We knew Dad would settle into the armchair in the living room for the rest of the day, with his cigarettes, the telly and his endless cups of tea. If we disturbed him we would be in for trouble. So we would sit on the kerb, like a little row of ninepins, with our dirty faces, grimy clothes and scuffed shoes, waiting for the other children to come out of their houses.

This was 1960, and the post-war building boom had not yet reached our corner of London. We lived in an area of the East End that seemed to be in a time-warp, neglected and forgotten. Cherbury Street, in the Borough of Shoreditch (which later became Hackney), was bleak and ugly, one of several identical streets which ran parallel to one another. It was lined with dilapidated Victorian houses, all full of families living in overcrowded and insanitary conditions. There were no trees or shrubs to alleviate its unrelenting grimness, nor were there any cars parked along the road – no one could ever have afforded one.

We shared one of these large, ugly houses with three other families. Like the rest of the street it should have been demolished years earlier and in fact it subsequently was, when the whole row of houses was pulled down and new flats built in their place. But when we lived on Cherbury Street, the whole place stank of decay, and the entrance hall and stairs were strewn with rubbish. Our flat was in the basement, where the five of us shared two rooms and a minute kitchen, with a toilet in the back yard. Very little light filtered in through the high, barred windows, and the whole place was damp, dingy and filthy. We children slept in the living room, Laurence and I on a put-you-up bed that had to be folded away during the day, and Kim on a cot in the corner. Our mattresses were saggy and ancient, and the bedlinen and blankets, thin, stained and old, offered little warmth or comfort. Our furniture was a hotch-potch of jumble other people had finished with. There were no curtains, nothing matched, and the few drawers there were had nothing in them anyway since none of us had more than a few items of clothing and no one bothered cleaning them or putting them away.

Once we three had been turfed out of the house there was nowhere for us to play apart from the bomb-sites, still not redeveloped, which surrounded us. These were supposed to be strictly out of bounds, but like the other children from our street we spent most of our time playing among the piles of rubble, bricks and broken glass. But we were not popular with the other kids. Even in conditions of such deprivation there was a pecking order, and we knew our place was right at the bottom. We were marked out from the moment we moved into the street. Before we had been there five minutes our parents had caused a scene. Mum had started chatting to the woman next door, and Dad, outraged that she was idling instead of making his tea, had come out and begun hitting and kicking her. He had dragged her back inside with curses and punches, laughing and telling the open-mouthed bystanders that she was a woman who needed taking in hand. Within a couple of weeks everyone knew that Ronald Ponting beat his wife Lilian up almost every day. Word would spread that there was a fight in our flat, and the children would gather round outside and laugh and shout insults.

If the three of us were outside when our parents started fighting we would try to hide. We desperately wanted the other kids to like us, but with our parents creating a public spectacle which horrified all the neighbours there was not much chance. From the beginning we felt different, the lowest of the low, and there was nothing we could do. Even as a small child I felt ashamed of the way my parents behaved. I longed for them to stop and behave normally like the other kids' parents, but there was little chance of that – they fought all the time and did not seem to care who heard them.

At the beginning there had been sympathy for Mum from the neighbours, and some of them had tried to step in and help; a few even called the police once or twice. But Dad soon sent them on their way, snarling at them to keep their noses out and telling the police it was a 'domestic' and that they were not needed. In the end everyone got used to hearing Lilian's shrieks and screams at all hours of the day and night, and sympathy gave way to exasperation. 'Why doesn't she get the 'ell out of it?' was a comment I heard many times.

The parents were, however, mostly sorry for us children. Sometimes one of the other mothers would put a comforting arm around us and give us a hug, or I would get a 'Chin up, Blondie' from one of the men. But mostly they just watched and tut-tutted from their front doors. I think we became a standing joke. Not many people had televisions, and I remember hearing a neighbour remark one day, 'Who needs a telly with the Pontings living here? They're all the entertainment we need.'

The children were just as unkind as some of their parents. They knew we were even worse off than them, and our unwashed and neglected state marked us out as much as our parents' awful scenes did. In our house there was no soap or shampoo, clothes were seldom clean and washing of any kind was a rare event. We smelled of dirt and decay, our hair was always tangled and our faces smeared in snot and dirt. The other kids would call us names: 'Smelly Pontings!' was their favourite taunt, and they would chant this at us over and over again. We would walk off and pretend we didn't care, trying to look defiant, but the constant rejection and teasing were awful.

We longed to be accepted and to join in the other kids' games, but this seldom happened. The most prized possession any child in our street had was a ball. With your own ball – carefully guarded and with your name written on it – other children came racing to play with you. But we had no ball, not even a chance of having one, and no one asked us to share theirs, so we were left to watch enviously as the others played catch or rounders or bad egg. Bad egg was a risky game; if you lost you had to walk through the arched arms of the other children, and they would punch and kick you. On the rare occasions that we were allowed to join in they made sure we lost and we got a good kicking. Another favourite game involved old prams, which were used as racing carts. As large numbers were needed we sometimes got to play this game with the others – although, of course, we were never the ones who got to sit in the prams and be pushed along.

Hunger was a permanent problem for us three kids. With nothing to eat most days until evening, we became little scavengers very early on. We would hang around other people's doors and sometimes one of the mothers would take pity on us and give us a piece of bread and dripping. But not often, because no one had much to spare.

We spent hours combing the bomb-sites and the surrounding streets and gutters for empty beer or lemonade bottles which we could take back to claim the penny deposit. On lucky days, when we had collected enough pennies, we bought delicious things called bottled jubblies from Rutter's, the local grocery shop. This was a magical place to us. Situated at the end of the road and nestled between a bagwash shop – the precursor to the launderette – and a newsagent's, it was full of wonders. Sawdust covered the floor and a large chiller cabinet took up most of the space inside. Behind the counter, in front of shelves of neatly stacked tins, stood the owner, a tall, dark man who always wore a crisp, white shirt with the sleeves rolled up to his elbows. Around his waist he would tie a heavy blue and white linen apron, and there was always a tea towel tucked into it to wipe his hands on after each customer had been served.

Taking centre stage on the counter was a large joint of ham. Sometimes we would watch, our mouths watering as we breathed in the beautiful smell, while the shop-keeper carved thick slices off the joint and placed them on a large piece of greaseproof paper, before weighing them and popping them into a brown paper bag for some fortunate customer. In an old freezer at the back of the shop there were small quarter-pint glass bottles of diluted orange squash. These were the jubblies, our favourite treats. On our lucky bottle days we would hand over our pennies and then carry the jubblies carefully down the street before sitting on the kerb outside our flat, scooping the iced orange out with a spoon and tipping it into our mouths.

On rainy days we had to find shelter wherever we could. Often we would creep upstairs in our house to see Mrs Casey. She was a tiny widow who lived in a single room on the first floor, surrounded by pictures of her dead husband. All she had was a bed, a small sofa and a table with two chairs. But she was kind and would often come to our aid, inviting us in, treating us to slices of toast and telling us all the local gossip.

At the end of the day we would see the other children collect at the bottom of the street to wait for their fathers to come home from work. The men would greet them with smiles, swinging the smallest on to their shoulders and ruffling the heads of the others. We three could only watch and wonder why our father never went to work or ruffled our heads. Why did our dad spend his days in front of the telly? Why was he not like the other dads, who looked friendly and seemed to like their kids? When we went inside for our tea there was no friendly chat, no catching up on the day or sitting down together to watch the telly. We would get whatever food there was in the kitchen – often just bread and jam or bread and dripping, with lots of salt to give it flavour – and then hope we could get through to bedtime without a beating, which meant staying out of Dad's way.

Dad beat us almost as often as he beat Mum. He would swear at us, lash out or kick us for no reason other than that he felt like it. When we were in the house with him we were like three silent little shadows, trying to make ourselves invisible in the pathetic hope of avoiding his wrath. But that was impossible. He would turn on us at the smallest excuse. If one of us failed to fetch him his cigarettes fast enough, put a cup down on his newspaper or simply did not get out of his way in time we would get a beating. He would use his hand, his belt, his shoe or anything else within reach, lashing out until his anger was spent. Beatings were part of everyday life, and none of us had any chance of fending him off. We would run around the room trying to escape, but it was useless. As blows rained down on me I felt like a rag doll with the stuffing knocked out of me, or a balloon being punched around the walls, with no will of my own.

When the beating was a bad one there came a point when everything blurred into one huge pain which I thought would never end. My natural reaction was to curl up on the floor, trying to cover my head with my arms as he towered over me, but it did not make a lot of difference. When he had vented his fury Dad would just walk away, leaving us in weeping, shaking little heaps on the floor, and sit down in his chair, shouting at Mum to make him a cup of tea as though nothing had happened.

After a beating I used to hurt all over. But Dad was clever. Although he injured us, we hardly ever ended up in hospital. There would be heavy bruises, cuts and sprains, but usually he stopped before it got worse than that. The injuries he did inflict were just ignored. Sometimes, if it was really bad, Mum would give us a plaster or a cold towel to hold over the hurt place, but even that was rare. If we cried, Dad would scoff that we were putting it on and tell us to shut up.

If anyone ever noticed an injury on one of us, we said nothing. Dad had sworn us to silence – the last thing he wanted was child protection officers sniffing about. He said if we told we would be sent to a children's home where life would be much worse than it was at home. Hard as this was to imagine, we believed him and kept our mouths shut. Nowadays any doctor who treated such injuries would alert social services to a possible case of child abuse. If subsequent investigations proved these suspicions to be correct, the child would probably be put in the care of foster-parents. But, forty years ago, things were not like that: no one asked questions, and on the rare occasions when one of us landed up in hospital we were just sent back home for further abuse.

Because their income consisted mainly of social security payments our parents relied on hand-outs for everything, apart from a few luxuries like the television which they got on hire-purchase. We children wished we could see the programmes other kids watched, like *Fireball XL5*, a great Gerry Anderson puppet show, *Hoppity*, or the magician David Nixon doing his card tricks, but Dad would never allow us to watch them. Mostly after tea we would be sent back outside until bedtime. On the rare evenings when Dad allowed us to sit in the living room and watch a programme with him it had to be his choice, which meant *Dixon of Dock Green*, *Z Cars* or *Scotland Yard*. As a small child I had no idea these programmes were fiction. Watching them, I assumed the police were so busy dealing with robberies and murders that they had no time to come and stop Dad hitting Mum and us kids.

Not for nothing was hire-purchase known as the never-never. A man would come to the door every week for the payments on the telly, and almost every time we children would be sent to make an excuse. When it was my turn I would stutter that my parents were out and the man would raise his eyebrows, sigh and say, 'Well, tell them it's three weeks they owe now – I'll be back.' I would nod and scurry inside, grateful to have got rid of him because it would mean Dad might be in a better mood. If the man persisted and threatened to come in and repossess the telly Dad would send Mum to pay him something, hoping that a token payment would do the trick. When he had had to part with money he would be in a bad mood for the rest of the day, which always meant a beating for Mum or us kids or both.

Dad spent most of the family's benefits on cigarettes and things for himself. There was no thought or logic to his spending. He would suddenly decide he wanted fancy electrical goods, some new gadget he had seen, like a device to cut crinkle chips, or a camera, and that would be the money gone for another week. There was never much left over for food. What groceries there were had to be bought on a daily basis, mainly because, like most of our neighbours, we never knew where the next few pennies were coming from, but also because we had no fridge. Fresh food was bought from the corner shop and eaten the same day, which was why we rarely had anything left for breakfast next day. On a good day Dad would feast on pork chops at teatime while the rest of us had mince or a cheap cut of meat, boiled potatoes and cabbage. On a bad day it was porridge or bread and dripping. There were a lot more bad days than good.

Things were not helped by the fact that Mum was a hopeless housekeeper. She could not cook so the food she made always tasted awful, and she had no idea how to manage on a small budget. She barely ever did any cleaning or laundry, and she seldom washed herself or any of us. Her whole life was spent trying to keep Dad happy. Her job was to keep us out of the way and get Dad whatever he wanted. And what he wanted more than anything was money. Time after time he would scream at her to find some money and push her out of the front door. She would come back hours later, worn out, with a ten-bob note in her hand (50p in today's money, and not worth that much even in the 1960s). Where she got it, we had no idea. It was not until much later that we understood what was going on.

Mum did not always leave the house when she needed to get money; sometimes men would come round to see her. Dad ignored them and stayed in the living room watching telly. Mum called the men 'uncles', and she would say, 'Uncle and I are just going into the next room for a chat.' The uncle would often give us a wink or a pat on the head, and sometimes the nice ones gave us a sweet. Then they would disappear, until a while later they would both reappear and the uncle would leave. At the time we did not think to question it. All we knew was Mum had got some money, and we were glad because that meant cigarettes for Dad and tea on the table.

Tall, with black hair slicked back and full of Brylcreem, Dad was stocky and powerful. He had a large hooked nose, broken years earlier, and an almost permanent scowl on his face. On the rare occasions when he did smile he revealed discoloured, chipped teeth which had not been cleaned for years.

Dad had been born tongue-tied – his tongue was attached by an extra piece of skin to the floor of his mouth, so that it lacked full movement. This left him with a speech impediment; his words, which came out in jerks and grunts, were unclear and he mumbled. He could not, for instance, say our names properly. Kim always sounded like 'Tim', Laurence was 'Orence' and I was 'Enny'. His disability also meant that there was always saliva around the outside of his mouth, and the spit would fly about when he spoke.

Our dad never opened his mouth without using a string of swear words. He only ever spoke to us in snarls and most of the time he did not use our names anyway – we would be 'You little cunts.' By the time we got to school we thought it was normal to use a sprinkling of expletives in every sentence and we did so too, until a few cuffs from the teachers taught us to keep our mouths shut in their presence.

As well as his speech problems Dad had fits. The story, which I learned when I got older, was that while stationed in India in the army he had fractured his skull in a fight and suffered brain damage. Dad's head injury was his excuse for everything: living off benefits, hardly ever working, and behaving like a brutal bully. When we were small the fits were frightening, but after a while we realised that Dad was faking. He could turn his fits on at will, whenever it suited him. If a debtor got too persistent, or someone started asking awkward questions, he would suddenly throw himself to the floor and froth at the mouth. We knew he was acting because the way he fell was too careful, and we would watch him squinting up at whoever was there to see if they had been taken in. Amazingly, they often were. Startled by Dad's sudden 'fit', they would usually beat a hasty retreat. But apart from those occasions which called for a fit, Dad was perfectly healthy. He never had one when the family was alone in the house.

Thanks to this talent for deception, most of the time Dad could get away with living on the army pension he received for his injuries and handouts from National Assistance intended for the support of his family. But every now and then poverty would force him to look for work and he would find a job in a factory or on an assembly line. When Laurence was born he was working in a bakery, and when I was born he worked for a while as a packer. But he would always leave the job within a few weeks, claiming it did not suit him or that he had been victimised, and go back into his old routine, chain-smoking in his armchair. And after a few years he gave up any pretence of working and settled down to a life on state handouts.

Despite his current sour appearance he had been fairly attractive as a young man, and he could still turn on the charm if it suited him. He played on his 'war wound' and plenty of people, believing that he had served his country and was a forgotten hero, would turn a blind eye to his appalling behaviour. Even the social workers who turned up from time to time were taken in. Dad would put on a great performance as the caring father, struggling to overcome his disabling fits and to bring up his children, and they would swallow the story and usually come up with some extra benefit or allowance to help him.

In contrast to Dad, Mum was a slight figure. In her youth she was pretty, with auburn hair and dark brown eyes, olive skin, a good bosom and long legs. She was reed-slim, no more than a size eight, but she had curves and her figure attracted admiring glances. In other circumstances she could have been a beauty, but her hair had been cropped short at Dad's insistence – he always cut it himself – and her face was hidden behind ugly, thick-rimmed glasses. When she went out she usually kept her head down, to hide the cuts and bruises on her face and to avoid the curious, pitying glances from her neighbours.

She sometimes wore mini-dresses when I was small – even after several children her figure was good and men would turn their heads to watch her. But in time she stopped wearing them and settled for a uniform of nylon slacks and a jumper, with down-at-heel plastic shoes and a grubby little apron with a pocket in it where she kept her secret stash of cigarettes. Like Dad she was a heavy smoker and she walked around with a cigarette glued to her bottom lip. Often the cigarette burned away without her taking a puff, and the ash on the end grew longer and longer but never fell off.

Mum had met Dad when she was nineteen and he was around twenty-four. They had jobs in the same factory and he had asked her out through a friend. In those days she had had long hair and wore contact lenses, and lots of the lads in the factory fancied her. But she chose Dad, and within ten days he had persuaded her to chop off her hair, swap the contact lenses for glasses and marry him. No one came to their wedding except Dad's best friend – their families were not even told about it until afterwards.

Broke and homeless, the newly-weds moved into a damp, dilapidated houseboat and thirteen months later Laurence came along. A year after that I was born, on 15 March 1956 in the City of London

Hospital. I was named Jeanette Lilian Ponting and I was a healthy 7lb 14oz – what they called a 'bonny baby' in those days. I have only found one picture of myself as a baby; any other photographs there might have been were lost long ago. That earliest picture is a small black and white snap of my brother and myself: I must have been around eight months and Laurence twenty-one months old. My mother is missing, but I am sure she was in the photograph, holding us on her lap. Someone tore her off; I have never discovered who or why. In another picture I am a little older, wearing a short double-breasted coat, white ankle socks and brown sandals. My haircut is the typical 'pudding-basin' of the time – straight fringe and short square bob. Laurence is standing beside me, his blond curls neatly smoothed, with an arm around me, already very much the big brother.

Kimberley was born two years after me. My father's parents, Sidney and Florence, organised a christening for the three of us in the local Methodist church. There were none of Mum's family there – they were Irish Catholics, and it was made clear by the Pontings that they would not be welcome.

From the start of their relationship Mum was totally under Dad's spell. He controlled her every move. It was as though from the moment they met he owned her and could do whatever he chose with her. No matter how many times he hit or humiliated her, she would never leave him. As little kids we would hear her sobbing in pain from another beating, then not long afterwards she would be giggling with him in the bedroom like a lovestruck teenager. Even at that young age it made no sense to me. Why would she laugh with him when he hurt her so much?

I have often wondered, looking back, whether Mum had some sort of learning difficulties. I might be wrong but if so, it might help to explain why Dad was able to keep his all-powerful hold over her and why she forgave him over and over again for his cruelty. Certainly Mum was child-like in all sorts of ways. She could not read or write much beyond a signature, and she would believe anything. She took old wives' tales very seriously. Ringing in the ears and a bird in the house both meant there would be a death, bubbles on your tea meant money coming, and to light three cigarettes from a single match was unlucky. She was always throwing salt over her shoulder to avoid bad luck – a sad little gesture, really, since her life seemed to be one long streak of bad luck. She was convinced she could talk to spirits and one day, when we were a little older, Kim climbed a tree and as Mum walked underneath she whispered, 'Lil Ponting . . . Lil.' Anyone else would have guessed it was a trick, but Mum wanted to believe it and even after Kim told her what she had done Mum was convinced she had a gift.

I think Mum cared for us, in her own way, but Dad was always her priority. When I was small I longed for affection from her. I wanted to cuddle up on her lap and smell her warm, safe smell. But that was never an option. If I tried to hug or kiss her she would gently push me away or tell me to go and play, and I soon gave up trying. The only affection between us was after she had suffered a beating, when we would try to comfort her and she might give us a brief hug. Apart from that she would sometimes hold our hands crossing a road, or give us a quick goodbye kiss on the cheek when she was off out, but that was it.

By the time I was four I already knew that we had to look after her, not the other way round. Mum looked to us to help her and would call out to us for help when Dad was beating her, even though we had no chance of helping her and it just meant that he would beat us too. Sometimes when that happened she would turn on him, shouting at him to leave us alone. 'They're only kids!' she would yell, as if that would make any difference to him. Later on I realised that sometimes she did try to protect us. She would shoo us out of the house when Dad was in a bad mood, knowing that she would get the beating and not us. I suppose it was her way of doing what she could.

While Mum was not one for hugs and affection, there were times when Dad liked to have cuddles and play games with us. But these were games I soon learned to dread. When he played them Dad had a funny look on his face and he would laugh in a strange way. One of his favourites was the children's rhyme 'This little piggy went to market'. He would count on our toes, saying:

> This little piggy went to market
> This little piggy stayed at home
> This little piggy had roast beef
> This little piggy had the bone
> And this little piggy went wee wee wee all
> the way home.

Lots of parents play this game with their children, tickling them under the arms at the end. But Dad's version was different. He went straight for our crotches and would tickle us there with his hard, rough fingers.

Another rhyme was:

> Walking round the garden
> Like a teddy bear
> One step, two steps
> And tickle you under there.

Again, his rough hands would dig into our private parts. When he did this I hated it. He hurt me and it felt all wrong – I knew the rhyme did not end like that. But when I said, 'No, Dad, you're s'posed to tickle under my arm' he would grin and do it again, digging even deeper into the tender place between my legs. I was much too afraid of him to protest.

Some mornings he would order us into his bedroom and make us play King of the Castle. He would lie in bed making a hill under the bedclothes with his bent knees, and bounce one of us up and down on top while he sang the rhyme:

> I'm the king of the castle
> Get down, you dirty rascal.

Then he would suddenly open his legs and we would fall between them. We did not enjoy the game very much because we were so scared of Dad, but we played along with it, unaware, at such a young age, that he was getting a sexual kick from our innocent writhings and tumblings. And although he sometimes made Laurence join in this game, Dad was always less interested in him than in Kim and me. Boys were just a nuisance as far as he was concerned; at least girls had their uses.

At the age of four I was able to escape for a few hours a day into a little world of order and calm when I was admitted to the pre-school class at Burbage Primary School in Hoxton, where Laurence was already a pupil. The building was large and bleak and looked like a workhouse. Very few children went to nursery or pre-school in those days, but this class had been established for the underprivileged children of parents who could not cope or whose children were left alone all day because their parents had to go out to work. Nearly every child there was badly dressed, hungry and neglected. But it meant I no longer had to hang around the streets all day. In the morning we played games, sang songs, drank our bottles of free school milk and had stories read to us, before being given a hot dinner and an afternoon nap on rows of little camp beds. I loved it. In fact the only thing I hated about pre-school was when the nit nurse, 'Nitty Nora' as we called her, arrived to inspect our heads for lice with a comb which she dipped in disinfectant and scraped along our tender scalps. Most of us had headlice most of the time, and our parents were asked to treat us with special shampoo. Ours never bothered.

One morning, not long after I had started at Burbage, the postman called. Few things interested Dad, but the arrival of post was one of them. It meant his giro cheque, and that meant cigarettes and money to spend, for a couple of days at least. But today the postman was calling at every house in the street to deliver the same letter. Soon clusters of women were gathering outside, buzzing with the news: we were all to be rehoused. We, the Pontings, had been offered a three-bedroom maisonette in Hoxton. This was enough to rouse Dad from his bed, and he shouted at Mum to get rid of us so that they could go down to the council offices to sign the papers.

'Quick,' Mum told us. 'Get your shoes on, I'm taking you to Auntie's.' We raced to put on our clothes while Mum fiddled with her glasses, broken again in that morning's beating and, in the absence of any Sellotape tried to mend them with an old bit of black masking tape. She found her purse and, peering through the one remaining lens in her glasses, struggled to count out the pennies for the bus fares.

At this point impatience got the better of Dad, who leaped up and snatched her purse from her, sending the few coppers she had in it rolling across the linoleum floor in all directions. He ordered her out of the room and the three of us perched on the edge of a chair, too scared to breathe, as he picked the money up and counted it out. This time we were lucky. He handed the money to Mum, and without another word she pushed us ahead of her out of the flat.

Outside, we children began to skip with excitement. We were going to Auntie's, and that was the best news possible. But Mum was tense. Dad would only allow her a certain amount of time to deliver us to Auntie's flat and get back to him. If she was late, it would mean another beating.

The walk to the bus stop was a familiar one. We

would walk to the end of the road and then cut through a block of flats. I loved this part of the journey. Although the flats were quite old they were in immaculate condition, and in the beautifully kept surrounding gardens the rose bushes filled the air with their wonderful scent. When a well-meaning neighbour stopped Mum to chat about the new house, her agitation increased. She excused herself, explaining that we had a bus to catch, and hurried on down through the flats, the three of us trotting at her heels.

It took half an hour on the bus from New North Road to Auntie's home just behind Highbury Corner in Islington. Just a short trip, but when we reached the other end we entered a different world.

2

Auntie

The hallway of Laycock Mansions, a large, pre-war block of flats, was always in semi-darkness and smelt of the carbolic disinfectant that Auntie, a stickler for cleanliness, regularly used to wash down the communal stairs and hallways. At the top of the stairs on the second-floor landing was her smart black front door with its familiar 'No Hawkers' brass plate fixed just above the letter-box. Mum would lean down and call out through the flap – Auntie was suspicious of strangers and would never open the door unless she knew who was there.

Seconds later we would be enveloped in her large, warm, familiar bosom, breathing in the scent of soap and lavender water and revelling in the hugs and kisses she showered on us. She would take us into her cosy, cluttered kitchen and make us mugs of milky tea in the special plastic cups she kept waiting for us on the dresser. Mine was yellow, Laurence's blue and Kim's pink. Then she would start to cook us a big meal.

Mum would only stay a few minutes – long enough for a muttered conversation with Auntie in the bedroom – before heading back to Dad. Although Mum was a grown woman and mother of three children, Auntie would insist on washing her dirty face and brushing her hair before she left. Sometimes Auntie would open the window and call Mum back, throwing down a handkerchief with money wrapped in it. Mum would catch it and shove it into her pocket, pausing for a quick smile of thanks before hurrying off.

Auntie's real name was Margaret Hinton. She was Mum's aunt and our great-aunt and, along with her husband Sid, had brought Mum up. Auntie loved to tell us stories about Mum when she was a little girl. Mum's own mother had died in childbirth and her policeman father, John, unable to cope on his own, had taken the little girl to his childless sister, who welcomed her with open arms. Auntie and Sid had lavished affection on little Lilian. They had never pretended to be her parents – her father had always visited every week and had doted on her. But they loved her and they made sure the little girl wanted for nothing. Auntie told us how Mum was given beautiful tailor-made clothes and every outfit she wore had matching shoes. Her long auburn hair was dressed in wonderful styles and she was taught perfect manners and taken on all kinds of outings, including trips to the theatre, music halls and, best of all, the Palladium, where all the top performers of the day appeared. When she was ten or eleven it was discovered that her eyesight was very poor. She was provided with glasses, which she wore at home, but Auntie and Sid also bought her contact lenses – hugely expensive in those days – so that her lovely brown eyes would not be hidden when she went out.

We loved these stories, though it was hard to equate them with the cowed, downtrodden figure we knew. It was not until we were much older that Auntie filled in the rest of the story. Soon after the end of the war, when Lilian was in her early teens, Sid was killed on his way to work one morning by one of the unexploded bombs that still littered London. Auntie was heartbroken. Sid had dreamed of a career for Lilian as a lawyer or a doctor, but she had struggled at school and she left with no qualifications. She did not need to work, but Auntie honoured a promise she had made to Sid to encourage Lilian to make her own way in the world. So Mum got a job on the assembly line in a local factory, and although it was dull she was excited about going out to work and earning money.

It was in this factory that Lilian had met Ronald Ponting. Soon afterwards she disappeared for ten days, at the end of which she arrived at Auntie's door with Ronald grinning behind her. Auntie had been shocked by Lilian's dramatically altered appearance. Her beautiful long hair had been hacked into a short, unflattering style and her contact lenses had been exchanged for ugly glasses. When the pair announced that they were married, Auntie's heart ached because she believed her niece had made a terrible mistake.

The young couple had already been thrown out by Ronald's parents after just a few days. They had gone to stay with Ronald's best friend, Laurie, but his parents too had asked them to move on. So, despite her misgivings, Auntie allowed them to stay, giving them her only bedroom and moving into the living room. When we were small Auntie was always careful in what she said to us about our father, but later on she told us how hard she had found it to accept him when Mum first brought him home. She had done her best, but despite her efforts she distrusted him from the start. She found him shifty and sinister and, if cleanliness was next to godliness, as she firmly believed, then it was clear to her that Ronald was definitely an atheist. After a few weeks the situation had become unbearable, so Auntie had loaned them the money to pay a deposit on rented accommodation. It was to be the first of many loans that she soon realised would never be repaid.

Lilian and Ronald then moved to the houseboat, and for the next year or so they had very little contact with Auntie. But a few weeks after Laurence was born Mum had arrived at Auntie's door with the baby, who she said had a cold. Laurence was clearly sick and it appeared that he had been left out in the rain in his pram after Dad had refused to let Mum bring him inside the boat. Auntie had melted at the sight of the baby, a beautiful child with a mop of thick curly blond hair, a small, pale face and large cornflower-blue eyes. Mum had deposited him there and gone back to Dad, while Auntie, who had nicknamed the infant Nobby, had taken him straight to a doctor. It turned out that he had pneumonia and it took Auntie several weeks to nurse him back to health.

A few weeks later Mum had turned up to take her baby back, and so a pattern was set which was to be repeated first with me and then with Kim and would last throughout our childhood. Whenever Dad wanted us out of the way we would be shipped off to Auntie's for days or even weeks at a time. Then, out of the blue, Mum would be sent to retrieve us, usually because Dad wanted to con more furniture or benefits out of Social Services and he needed to convince them he was struggling to bring us up.

Dad knew that Auntie adored us and he used us as a weapon to get money out of her. Every now and then Auntie would refuse to cough up any more money and Dad would promptly threaten that she would never see us again. It hurt her, but she was no pushover. Sometimes she would stick to her guns, knowing that Dad would soon get sick of the 'brats' hanging around and needing to be fed, and send us back to her. In the intervening weeks she missed us terribly, but her 'babies' always arrived back eventually, hungry, filthy and in desperate need of her warm and loving care. Auntie had always refused to set foot in Mum and Dad's home. She knew that, despite her efforts to teach Mum housekeeping skills, her niece had absolutely no idea how to manage, and that under Dad's disastrous influence the pair of them lived like tramps. But it was one thing to know this and another to see it for herself. To witness the squalor in which we children lived would have been too much for her, and in any case Dad had made it clear that she was not welcome.

Our only 'real' grandparents, Nanny and Grandad Ponting, were very different from Auntie: they were distant figures who never featured strongly in our childhood. Grandad worked hard and the family were fairly well off, living in the top half of a big house which they shared with Grandad's brother Walter and his wife May, who lived in the bottom half. Grandad was a kindly figure who seemed fond of us. But he was ruled by Nanny, who was disapproving and clearly found us little more than a nuisance.

Dad was the eldest of their three boys, and when he was younger his parents had had high hopes for him. I recall my father telling me he had been asked to join in a business with Grandad, but Dad showed little interest in working for them or anyone else, and they were bitterly disappointed. By the time he had been discharged from the army — dishonourably, so rumour had it — they had given up any hope of him doing well at anything. And when their Methodist son married a Catholic girl who was barely literate and wouldn't say boo to a goose they more or less washed their hands of him.

Every now and then Dad would take us over to visit them. Grandad would smile and pat our heads but then slip away to his garden shed, and Nanny would only allow us into the kitchen where we sat at the table with a drink. If we were lucky, Grandad would say, 'Why not give them a biscuit?' before he disappeared, and Nanny would reluctantly produce one. From the kitchen we would catch glimpses of their severe-looking front room, where all the furniture was covered in plastic, big, heavy drapes hung at the windows and a huge sideboard housing a drinks cupboard and gramophone stood along one wall. After our drink we would be allowed to go and say hello to Uncle Walter and Aunt May downstairs, which was more fun. They were kinder to us, although we were still only allowed into their kitchen, and there was the added attraction of

Uncle Walter's glass eye. He liked to take it out and put it on a plate and say, 'It's watching you', which fascinated and horrified us at the same time.

The joint christening of us three children was the last time the Pontings splashed out on our behalf. Apart from our rare, uncomfortable visits, the only contact we had with them was a birthday card which usually had some money in it – and Dad always swiped this before we got it. He would steam open the envelope, remove the cash or postal order and then make a vain attempt to reseal the envelope. It was so obvious it had been tampered with. The only other contribution they were willing to make to their feckless son's household was a weekly carrier bag of their left-over fruit, vegetables and broken biscuits, which Dad would collect from their kitchen door every Friday, like a beggar.

What a contrast was our relationship with Auntie. To the three of us her small flat was a palace filled with treasures and delights. It was clean, warm, comfortable and safe – everything our own home was not. We all had our special nicknames: Laurence was still Nobby, I was Jinnybelle and Kim, who was the spitting image of Mum, with her olive skin and dark hair, was Auntie's little Black and Tan.

Every time we came to stay Auntie would begin by giving the three of us a thorough wash. Each one in turn would be lifted on to the wooden draining board in the kitchen, where we would sit with our feet in the big butler sink. There was only cold running water from the single tap, so she would boil a kettle and pour it into the cold water in the sink and then wash us before changing us into clean clothes. At Auntie's we looked clean, cared for and respectable. She hardly ever sent clothes back with us when we returned home, because she knew they would soon become filthy and tattered or be sold off for cigarette money. Instead she kept them washed, ironed and neatly folded in the large drawers of her old-fashioned wardrobe, ready for us to wear when we were with her.

Auntie herself was always immaculately turned out. By the time I was four she was almost sixty, but she had been a 'looker' in her youth and still enjoyed taking trouble over her appearance. Every morning she would sit at the dressing table in her bedroom and put her long, wavy, red hair up, gathered at the centre and fanning out into a perfect doughnut-shaped bun on the top of her head. Her make-up would be carefully applied: blue eye-shadow, pencilled-on brows and pink lipstick. If there was a stray hair on her chin we would watch in fascination as she took out a round stick of wax, melted the top over a candle, stuck it on her chin and yanked the offending hair out. Auntie taught us that you should always be nice and clean and that it was important to add something to yourself by creating your own smell. Her favourite had always been lavender water and she splashed it on liberally, so that we came to associate the clean, sweet smell with her.

The story of her youth was a colourful and romantic tale that we loved to hear over and over again. She had been born in 1901, one of thirteen children of Irish parents who had emigrated to England in the hope of a better life. Auntie had danced the charleston, worn the daring flapper dresses of the 1920s and enjoyed the attentions of plenty of eager young men. She had been sent out to work at an early age and had got a job in a factory ironing clothing with a huge, heavy press. But even though she had had to leave school to bring in income for the family, her parents had continued to educate her at home and she had become a good reader and writer. She had met Sid, her future husband, on the tram as they both travelled to work. His job was in the print industry in Fleet Street and he would tell her the headlines for the day, or what stories were about to break. Auntie adored Sid from the start, and despite their childlessness they were very happy together.

When we were children Auntie's smart dresses and skirts were always covered by a blue nylon overall. It buttoned up the front and had deep pockets in which she kept an assortment of matches, clothes pegs, keys and other paraphernalia. She wore her overall both in and out of the house and it was as much her trademark as the red bun on top of her head, though in winter the overall would be covered by her favourite red coat with its smart fur collar. Everyone in the area knew Auntie, and they knew how much she loved us children and how happy she was when we were with her. Neighbours, shopkeepers and stall-holders in the local market would wave, smile and stop for a chat with us as Auntie did her rounds for the day's shopping and we trotted happily behind her.

She was a house-proud woman and her flat was always spick and span, with every piece of furniture and all the windows polished until they shone. Washing had to be done by hand in the large bathtub, using water heated by the large gas-fired geyser on the bathroom wall. After that the clean washing was first run through the mangle which stood next to the bath and then hung on lines across the bathroom – Auntie would never have dreamed of hanging her 'smalls' outside. When everything was dry she ironed it on her big kitchen table with a heavy flat-iron which she heated over the stove, testing the temperature by spitting on it until the spit sizzled and evaporated. Even our knickers and socks were neatly pressed, and our dresses were hung away in her big wardrobe on silky padded hangers.

Our favourite room in Auntie's flat was the

kitchen. Seated at the big table, next to the dresser where all the plates, cups, knives and forks were kept, we would help Auntie to prepare the vegetables for supper. On top of the dresser was a silver egg-cup where she kept her shillings for the electric meter. On a table by the small cooker stood a wireless, which Auntie would listen to while she cooked or did the washing up. The wireless had two huge knobs and a row of push buttons on it; a panel in the front, which lit up when the thing was switched on, hid the speaker. Auntie liked the Home Service, which played musical requests for troops stationed abroad, or the Light Programme, which played all her favourite tunes by stars like Andy Williams and Billy Cotton. When the Light Programme started to use fast-talking disc-jockeys like Simon Dee and Jimmy Young, and to play more up-to-date pop music like the Beatles and Cliff Richard, Auntie switched off. She'd say, 'That's naughty – it's too modern' and turn over to something more traditional.

Every morning Auntie got up at five to begin her preparations for the day, leaving the three of us curled up fast asleep in the big double bed we all shared with her. By the time we had woken she had already dressed, cleaned the flat, done the washing and prepared breakfast. At Auntie's the food was delicious and there was plenty of it, although all she had to cook on was a two-ringed cooker similar to the one we had in Cherbury Street. On schooldays Auntie would have us up early, dress us and give us boiled eggs and dip-dip soldiers for breakfast. She would say, 'Let's give your shoes a spit and polish', and they would be rubbed to a perfect shine. We would clean our teeth with the toothbrushes she kept for us; we each had one which matched our mug. Before we left to catch the bus we would be lined up next to the front door for inspection, so that she could make sure our clothes, hair and faces were perfectly clean and we were looking our very best.

Of course our teachers at pre-school, and later those at school, noticed the enormous difference between the way we looked when our parents sent us and our neatly turned out appearance when we were staying with Auntie. They never said anything to us, but we could see that they liked Auntie, knowing that she cared for us and gave us some love and stability. She became a familiar sight around the school, bustling along in her overall or her red coat, stopping to say hello to the other mothers.

Every now and then when Auntie took us to school or collected us Mum would turn up at the school gates. She had not come to see us, though – she had come to ask Auntie for money. As soon as she had it she would give us a quick peck on the cheek and hurry back to Dad waiting impatiently at home. We were relieved when Mum left without taking us back. We wanted to stay with Auntie more than anything – we dreaded Mum taking us back home again. Home meant beatings, hunger, dirt and fear. Home meant Dad.

Laurence and I were envious of Kim when she was still young enough to stay with Auntie all day. It was not that we hated school, but a day with Auntie was much nicer. Even the chores, like scraping new potatoes and popping peas, were fun with Auntie.

But when the holidays and weekends came we really loved it. On these days we could snuggle down in the big bed a little longer before setting off with Auntie on all kinds of adventures. We would go on days out to the seaside or shopping trips, or buy Red Rover bus tickets which allowed us to go anywhere in London.

On Saturdays Auntie often took us to visit her sister Mary, who lived up the Holloway Road. None of us liked Aunt Mary. She made no attempt to hide her hostility and made it quite clear that she thought her sister should not be spending so much time and money on us. Her welcome was grudging at best, but she lived in a large, gloomy house that we found fascinating, so we would disappear to explore its many spooky corners while Auntie and Aunt Mary had tea together.

Afterwards we would get back on the bus and

carry on up the Holloway Road to Highgate, cling-
ing on to our seats and squealing in terror as it
struggled up the last part of the steep hill. But
somehow it always managed to reach the top,
where we got off next to the village green. In
Highgate there was a shop where Auntie bought
cheese and butter, and we would watch wide-eyed
as a man in a white overall and cap deftly and
speedily moulded the butter into shape using two
wooden spatulas. After that it would be wrapped in
greaseproof paper and weighed – we could never
work out how he managed to produce a perfect
half-pound every time.

Close by was our favourite landmark, a stone
surrounded by metal railings in the shape of a
birdcage. Sitting on top of the stone was a black
cat, and it was said that this was the exact spot
where Dick Whittington was told to turn around
and return to London. We loved to hear the story of
the boy who had come to seek his fortune and who
became the city's first Lord Mayor. At the back of
the village there was a large park where, after the
shops, we would head for a walk. It had a pond
where children sailed their toy boats and Laurence,
who had a passion for model boats and longed to
own one, would spend ages watching them.

When we managed to drag him away we would
carry on to the pathway which took us through the
woods to Kenwood House, a beautiful eighteenth-

century stately home which stood regally before a lake, surrounded by immaculate gardens full of flowers. To one side of it was a coach-house which had been turned into a tea shop, and the three of us would clamber aboard the replica of an old-fashioned coach which stood outside while Auntie went in to buy sandwiches and drinks. Beside the lake was a picnic area, reached by a small wooden bridge. This was one of our favourite spots, and sometimes Auntie would bring a picnic lunch which we would eat sitting at one of the wooden tables. After lunch we would wander through the house, which was open to the public and housed many wonderful works of art. I would stare for hours at the paintings of landscapes and beautiful figures, lost in their beauty.

Back in the park, at the right time of year we would run down the grass verges to the rows of abundant blackberry bushes which grew there, and pick bags of fruit for Auntie to bake into a pie. At the end of the day, tired and happy, we would clamber back on the bus and sing songs while she chatted to fellow passengers. Back at home Auntie would prepare our favourite meal: steak and kidney pudding, chips and baked beans, all washed down with milky tea in our special mugs, while Auntie sipped hers from a bone china cup and saucer. After we had helped Auntie wash and dry the dishes and replace them on the dresser we would go through to the living room, which always smelled of Auntie's favourite crystallised air fresheners in little plastic holders which she hung liberally around the flat. At the back of the living room was a large sofa, and fresh, snowy white net curtains and heavy drapes hung at the windows.

The most exciting thing in Auntie's flat was the huge old glass-fronted cabinet which stood in the corner of the living room. Its doors were always locked and Auntie kept the key in the pocket of her overall. We would beg her to let us open it, but she never would, so instead we would peer past our reflections in the polished glass to the treasures inside. On the top shelf was an exquisite silver tea and coffee set on a silver tray. I used to stare at the small pair of silver sugar tongs for hours, imagining what it would be like to use them. On the next shelf down there were porcelain statuettes, wonderfully detailed, of women in flowing dresses and men in their finery; I used to wonder whether they had been real people once. On the bottom shelf were two huge oriental vases, several other pieces of china and a willow pattern tea set.

On the wall was a picture of Uncle Sid, whom we thought very handsome, and a crucifix with a sculptured scroll on the top. Auntie's Catholic beliefs were still important to her. She loved hymns, and we knew that she kept her rosary beads in a drawer in the kitchen.

In the corner of the living room was a television set and in front of it a small two-seater sofa and a chair. This was where we all settled to watch our favourite shows, Laurence and me on the sofa and Kim curled up on Auntie's lap in the chair. We loved *The Andy Williams Show* and *The Black and White Minstrel Show*, but our favourite show was Billy Cotton's *Bandstand*, with its glamour, sparkle and jolly tunes. When it was over Auntie would get us into our pyjamas and we would kneel beside the bed and say our prayers. Mine were always the same: 'Please don't let us go back home. Let us stay at Auntie's for ever.'

After prayers Auntie would tuck us all into her big bed and sing us songs or hymns in her high, sweet voice, or tell us stories about the war and happy times with her beloved Sid. Sometimes Laurence was allowed to stay up a little bit longer, and then Kim and I would lie in bed playing 'scratch, rub and tickle', rubbing and tickling each other's backs until we fell asleep. I would always make Kim do my back first and, much to her indignation, often fell asleep before she got her turn.

On Sundays Auntie would dress us in our very best clothes. Kim and I would wear dresses with matching jackets, ankle socks which Auntie had boiled to snowy perfection, and shiny black patent shoes. Laurence would wear a crisp white shirt and long trousers, which made him feel very grown-up. Dressed and ready, we would set off for Chapel Street Market. It was a mile away and we always walked, so that Auntie could enjoy the admiration of passers by as they spotted her beautifully dressed little brood. At the market we would head for the fruit and veg stall, where Auntie would choose her produce with meticulous care, examining every apple and sprout for a hint of imperfection. Once she was satisfied we would move on to the Jewish butcher's. Auntie had a passion for sweetbreads, and the owner knew her well and would give her the best he had. We would finish up at the Italian ice cream parlour, where we would each be bought a huge cornet filled with different flavours of ice cream.

After our tour of the market we would head home again and we children would often put on a play or a show for Auntie in the living room. We would dress up in old clothes that she had saved for us and sing songs we had heard on the TV, while Auntie would cheer and whistle loudly. Sometimes her brother Fred and his wife, Aunt Ninny, would call round, sit through our shows and give us half a crown (12½ p) at the end. On Sunday evenings we had the biggest treat of all – Auntie's Ding Dong Rockabilly. This consisted of Neapolitan ice cream sandwiched between two wafers, with chopped up Mars Bar, Maltesers or Galaxy chocolate and chopped fresh fruit on top, all washed down with cream soda. It was heaven.

We never wanted our time at Auntie's to end, but it always did, usually without any notice. We would be hauled away by Mum with no time for more than a quick hug with Auntie and no idea when we would see her again. Two weeks after depositing us there so that she and Dad could claim their new council home, Mum arrived to collect us. My heart sank when I heard her call through the door. I dreaded the walk to the bus stop, knowing that Dad would be waiting at the other end and all the horror, pain and misery would start again. But there was no choice: Auntie could not keep us, much as she wanted to.

We heard Mum telling her how nice the new maisonette was and that this would be a fresh start for the whole family. Auntie, trying to sound enthusiastic, said she hoped it would make a difference. We children were full of curiosity. Were we really going to leave the horrible dirty flat and go to a new home? Would it be clean and nice, like Auntie's? Mum promised us our own bedrooms – no more sleeping in the living room. We were a little scared at the idea of somewhere we had never been before, but excited too. My small heart filled to bursting with the hope that now everything would be different and that having a nice, clean, proper home would please our father. If Dad was happy he might be nice to us, and Mum might have time to give us cuddles like Auntie did, and maybe we would even have enough food to eat.

As we trailed down the stairs behind our mother I turned to see Auntie standing outside her door watching us go. She was still smiling, but there were tears in her eyes.

3

New Hopes, New Fears

We had never seen anything as smart, shiny and clean as our new home. We three children ran from room to room examining everything with gasps of amazement. Monteagle Court was a brand-new block of sixteen maisonettes a few streets away from our old home, not far from busy Hoxton Market and just off the main Kingsland Road which ran from Stoke Newington through to the City. Our flat had its entrance on the ground floor. Next to the shiny new mustard-coloured door with its brass number three was a coal bunker. For us this was a very modern development: the coalman would be able to make his delivery without coming inside the house, and we could reach the coal from another small door inside the hallway.

Inside, the walls were all freshly painted a lovely cream colour. Off the hall was the kitchen, which housed all kinds of wonders. There was a sink so shiny that I thought it was made from solid silver. It had two taps, not just the one we were used to, which meant there would be hot running water – a luxury we had never come across before. There was also a huge larder, with a stone floor and walls to keep everything cool, and kitchen units with cupboards and drawers. Best of all there was a small fridge set into the wall, where we would be able to keep our milk to stop it going sour. Across the hallway, opposite the stairs, was the toilet. An inside toilet was a luxury we had previously experienced only at Auntie's. Now we would have our own. Kim was barely out of nappies and too young to be impressed, but Laurence and I were as pleased as if we had won the big prize at a fair.

At the end of the hall was a large living room, with a door leading to a small balcony which overlooked the grassed area at the back of the block. The living room had a fireplace with a gas tap in it. This would make lighting the fire much easier – no more need for fiddly, messy firelighters. Like all the other maisonettes, ours had three bedrooms. This meant that Kim and I had a room to share and Laurence had his own little bedroom, which pleased him enormously as he was already an intensely private child who liked to spend hours alone. Mum and Dad took the biggest bedroom, which was at the front, next to an outside flight of stairs which people used to reach the flats on the first floor. As well as the bedrooms there was also a bathroom upstairs, painted a lovely blue and containing a shiny white bathtub and a basin.

All our furniture from the old flat had been brought over and installed, but even the grubby, tatty state of those few items failed to detract from the delights of our new home. And there were some extras: Dad's parents had given us a smart new table and chairs, and the council had provided beds for us children. Kim's and mine were arranged neatly side by side in our room, alongside an old chest of drawers and a built-in wardrobe. The floors were bare, but the council were going to provide carpets and linoleum, as well as curtains and a new cooker, all due to be delivered the next day. This was the main reason Dad had wanted us around during the move. We were useful in his bid to get as much out of the authorities as he could.

It was hard not to believe, as we lay in bed that first night with all this newness around us, that things would not get better. Dad seemed pleased with the new house: would it be enough to stop him attacking Mum and the three of us? Would it mean that we could wash and have clean clothes and stop being the smelly Pontings? Would it mean there was more food on the table? I wished with all of my scared little four-year-old's powers of wishing that it would.

My dreams were short-lived. The next morning we woke to the sounds of Dad beating Mum and Mum screaming, 'Help me! Get him off me!', just like always. We children cowered in our bedrooms, our hands over our ears, our stomachs churning with terror. I felt desolate – it seemed that nothing was going to change after all.

The beatings he inflicted on us three went on too. And Dad had invented a game he loved to play which gave those beatings a whole new twist. He would line us up and force us to take all our clothes off. We would have to stand in front of him naked, not moving a muscle, while he shouted at us. Then suddenly hc would lash out and start to hit us. We would stand there trembling, covered in cuts and bruises from his previous bouts of violence, while he punched us with his fist, one finger crooked outwards so that it hurt us more. Hc would poke, pinch and slap us too, enjoying himself as he did so. We would stand there with tears pouring down our cheeks, saying, 'Sorry, Dad. Sorry, Dad', even though we usually had no idea what we were supposed to have done wrong. Often Laurence would own up to something just to stop his sisters being subjected to this torture. Kim and I would be dismissed and Laurence would take the beating alone, but in our eyes a real hero.

Sometimes Dad would pick on just one of us, and after we had stripped he would make us stand on a chair in the middle of the room. If we moved he would hit us. Not long after we moved into the new house it was my turn for this particular torture. I had put a cup down on his newspaper, leaving a wet ring there. Dad was incandescent with rage. He made me take my clothes off, slapped me on my back, bottom and stomach, then stood me on a chair, naked and freezing, and left me there. The pain and the cold were awful and I started shaking as shock set in. I needed the toilet, and after a while I began to wet myself. When Dad saw he exploded with rage and began punching, poking and hitting me, swearing at the top of his voice and calling me a 'fucking little cunt'. He made me stand there for the rest of the evening.

When finally I was allowed to drag myself up to bed, clutching my bundle of clothes to my chest, I was shaking so badly I could not even get my vest and pants back on. I crawled under the covers and curled into a ball. My whole body hurt, the urine had made my legs sting and I was hungry and very cold. But more than anything I was terrified he would come after me again. Kim climbed into bed with me and cuddled up to give me some extra warmth. We did not dare make a sound in case he heard it. As Kim fell asleep I cried silent tears until I too fell into an exhausted sleep.

Within a few weeks our new home was begin-ning to lose its shiny-clean feel and a layer of dirt had settled over everything. Mum never had much idea of how to keep things clean and she seemed not to notice. In any case she was far too busy trying to please Dad. I wished our flat was clean and smelled nice, like Auntie's. But there was nothing I could do about it; my little attempts to tidy up or clean anything made no impact.

Getting outside was the best escape from the squalor and from Dad, and we children were out every day, exploring our new surroundings. The front of our block faced on to a small street called Hare Walk. At the end was a pub called the Standard, which had an off-licence next door where Dad would send us for cigarettes or to return empty bottles. The Standard faced on to Kingsland Road. Across the street from the pub were two red telephone boxes which everyone in our block used to make their calls, including the ones we kids or our neighbours made to the police when Dad's beatings got out of hand.

Next to the phone boxes was the Geffrye Museum, which soon became a place of refuge for me. Children were not supposed to go in without an adult, but I often managed to sneak in and if that was not possible then just being in the beautiful grounds was enough. The museum contained exhibitions of life through the ages: whole scenes and rooms from times past were re-created inside it, using life-sized models. I especially liked the Victorian ones and those from the world wars, and would stand and gaze at them for hours. In the gardens next to the museum was a playground, set on a concrete platform. Children were allowed to use it when they went in with their parents, but we discovered a secret door in the wall next to the museum building which led straight to it. Not many people realised the door was there, and we children kept it a secret. The playground housed a sandpit, an old bus, a set of swings, a slide and a roundabout. Our favourite game was Drop the Lolly Stick – we would lie on the roundabout as it spun round, attempting to pick up a lolly stick lying on the ground.

Close to our block of flats was another, called the Geffrye Estate, and beyond this was a corrugated iron fence which separated the flats from a crumbling, disused factory. To one side of the factory was a small parade of shops. Mrs Evans, a gentle lady who always wore a white overall and spoke with a strong Welsh accent, ran the grocery shop. This was next to the newsagent's, run by Pat and Ted. They were nice, but the shop was old and musty and we preferred another sweet shop up the road which we called the blue shop, because of its blue-painted front. The blue shop was run by a lovely, kind lady called Dolly, and to us it was the best shop in the world. We would go in there whenever we had a few pennies to spend and Dolly would make up a mixed bag for us, containing black jacks, flying saucers, pear drops, pink shrimps, sherbet dib-dabs and white chocolate mice.

If you walked on up Kingsland Road you came to St Leonard's Hospital, and if you crossed Nuttall Street, up on the left you would find a dingy little grocery shop. It was run by a middle-aged husband and wife who were happy to sell you anything at any time of the day or night; if the shop was shut you knocked on their door and one of them would let you in. We were often sent there, when other shops were shut, to get cigarettes or milk. In those days packets of Brooke Bond tea had orange stamps on the side, which you could cut out and stick on to a card. It took a lot of stamps to fill the card, but when it was full it was worth five shillings (25p) worth of groceries. We usually swapped ours at Mrs Evans's shop, but out of hours we could swap it for cigarettes in Nuttall Street.

Beyond our flats in the other direction were a green space and two more blocks of flats, called Cordelia House and Rosalind House. If you walked between these two blocks you would come to a small path which led through an alleyway to Hoxton Market. This was a thriving street market in those days, with busy stalls up both sides of the street. On the corner of the alleyway which led to the market was a shoe shop. It sold the cheapest possible shoes, and this was where we were always taken to get new school shoes when our parents got the state clothing allowance. Close to the shoe shop was the undertakers, Hayes and English, and beyond that a Woolworth's.

There were eight pubs in the street and the most popular was the Bacchus Arms, right in the middle of the market. Next to it was Fortune's pie and mash shop. Dad had forbidden us to go there, telling us it was a nasty place full of scum. He thought that forbidding us to go showed that we had standards – which of course it didn't at all. And his ban failed to stop us. We loved Fortune's, where for two pennies you could have a bowl of mash and liquor. This was mashed potato with a hollow in the middle that would be filled with a green parsley sauce known as liquor – goodness knows why. We would get one bowl and three spoons and sit on the wooden benches at the tables in the small room at the back, taking turns to dip into the bowl. For a shilling (5p) you could have a whole hot meal of pie and mash. It was not often that we had riches like that, but on the rare occasions when we did we would revel in the smell of delicious hot pie. After handing over our money we would cover our food in malt vinegar, salt and pepper before tucking in.

The jeweller's was one of the most popular shops in the market – not because anyone bought jewellery, but because it was also a pawn shop. The familiar three brass balls outside could be seen from the end of the street and there was always a queue outside. The shop would take almost anything, as long as they could get something for it. Mum often went down there. I remember her pawning Dad's winter overcoat, the iron and the kettle.

Mum used to take us down to Hoxton Market most days to get whatever food we could. We would wait behind her, Kim in a big old Silver Cross pram which had seen better days and Laurence and I standing beside it, while she wheedled and pleaded to get credit from the fruit and veg stalls for a few spuds or carrots. We would watch the men sitting at tables on the paved area outside the Bacchus Arms, drinking their pints of bitter, while the children would get packets of Smith's crisps, with the salt wrapped separately in a small blue twist of paper inside. One day, while Mum was busy at one of the stalls, one of the men outside the pub got up and came over to us. I was a grubby four-year-old, standing beside the pram in jelly shoes with no socks, which were hurting my feet, and wearing a faded little dress. He was a big man and he was wearing a beautiful suit, with shiny shoes and dark, gleaming, slicked back hair. He bent down and picked me up to give me a cuddle, saying, 'Who are you, then?' Then he sat down again with me on his lap and bounced me up and down before putting me into the pram beside Kim, giving me a squeeze and tucking a five pound note into my hand.

I heard someone say to Mum, 'That's Reggie Kray – he's just lost his wife,' but of course the name meant nothing to me then. It was only years later that I realised I had been given a cuddle by one of the East End's most infamous villains. Reggie Kray and his twin brother Ronnie were gangsters who ran rackets all over the East End and were regarded with awe, respect and fear by people in the area. Hoxton was at the centre of the territory they ruled over. I have sometimes wondered whether Reggie's moment of tenderness towards me came about because he had a genuine affection for children. A few years later he and his brother were convicted of murder and jailed for life.

The Krays were not the only villains in the area, of course. It was not long after we moved into Monteagle Court that Dad's 'games' started to go further. He would order us into his bedroom in the mornings, while Mum was downstairs making his breakfast. The bedroom was always gloomy because the curtains were kept permanently drawn so that people passing by on the staircase outside could not see in. Like every other room in the flat it was full of overflowing ashtrays, and on top of the smell of stale cigarettes it had a sour, sickly stench which we hated. He would play his old favourite, King of the Castle, with Kim and me. We would go through the motions like little wooden robots, praying it would soon be over. Dad had no interest in Laurence when it came to these games, and Kim and I still had no idea what kind of pleasure Dad got from them.

But that was only the beginning. Soon he started ordering me into the bedroom on my own in the mornings and playing games that frightened me. He would say he wanted a 'cuddle', with the same funny look on his face he always had when we played his games. Then he would take me in under the bedcovers and make me take off my knickers and vest, rubbing me with his large, rough hands or pulling me against him. At the same time he would tell me to hold his penis and rub it. I did not like the feel of this big, hard thing, I was not sure what it was, but I knew it was part of him and I hated touching it. But almost as bad as that was the smell of him. His body had a rank, dirty odour which made me feel sick, and his breath as he put his face close to mine stank of stale tobacco and sour milk. I was desperate to get out from under the covers and away from him, but I did not dare ask to go. I would lie there, rigid and terrified, waiting for him to tell me I could go, or for Mum to arrive with his breakfast, when I could run back to my own room and hide there.

Mum never seemed surprised to see me there, even if I was in the bed with no clothes on. He would just say, 'Jenny came in for a cuddle', and Mum would say, 'Oh, right' and then carry on as usual. I think I knew then that she was never going to help me or stop him. If she understood what he was doing – and she would have to have been blind not to – she did not let on. I suppose her own fear of him was greater than her need to protect her children. But for me it was one of many betrayals, one of those times when an adult could and should have helped me, yet did nothing.

One morning, after one of Dad's 'games' sessions which had ended with him punching me in the face because he thought I was not cooperative enough, I was sent out to play as usual. I was scavenging around the waste ground near the factory when I found a broken piece of mirror. When I looked into it I saw a grey-faced little girl with blood on her nose and hair so tangled where it had been pulled that no brush would go through it. My neck was filthy and tears and dirt stained my face. Looking at myself, my eyes narrowed. I hated everyone. I felt let down and hurt and angry. But I knew I was not beaten. I was still here, and as I gazed up to the sky I made a solemn promise that I would survive.

4

Nightmares

A week before the new school term started we were sent back to Auntie's. Dad had decided there was no more to be got out of social services for a while and had tired of having us around, so he ordered Mum to take us to 'that old bag', as he called Auntie. It often happened that we were sent to Auntie's just before a new term, because our parents knew she would clean us up, get us ready for school and buy us the new clothes and shoes we needed. We children were just happy to be back in the familiar comfort and safety of her flat.

For me the relief at getting away from Dad was even greater now that he had started his nasty games in the bedroom. At Auntie's I could pretend there was no Dad, no fear, no lying rigid in the bed while he pawed me. I was safe. I never told her what Dad did. In fact we never talked about him when we were with her. It was as though we wanted to be as far away from the misery of home as possible. I wanted to feel safe and warm and good and be Auntie's precious little Jinnybelle, and telling her about Dad might have spoiled that. And perhaps deep down I knew, too, that there was nothing Auntie could do to help.

On this visit Auntie told us we were in for a really special treat. I was about to start proper school, rather than just pre-school, and she had decided that in honour of the occasion I must have a new dress from a smart shop. Selfridge's was, and still is, one of London's largest and grandest department stores, situated right in the heart of the West End, in Oxford Street. To us it was a wonderful place, full of magical things. Usually Auntie saved the trip for Christmas and we would go there to see Santa Claus in his grotto. Coming for an extra visit was as good as an outing to the seaside.

Every time we went I would wander through the store as if in a dream, watching the intoxicatingly perfumed, glamorously dressed women who swanned through the revolving doors and along aisles laden with more beautiful and exotic things than I had ever imagined existed. I used to wish that I could lock the feeling I experienced there – the excitement and wonder – in a bottle that I could take home and uncork when I felt sad or lonely. After we had browsed through the departments, picking out a pretty dress for me on our way, Auntie took us to the enormous food hall where she bought us little individual loaves of Hovis bread and a small portion of smoked salmon for a special tea when we got home.

The next few days, until school started, were spent swimming in the Highbury Fields pool, not far from Auntie's flat. She would take a picnic lunch and sit watching while we splashed and played for hours. In the evenings we would go back to the safe, warm sanctuary of the flat, snuggle next to her on the sofa with our night-time Ovaltine and pray that we never had to go home again. But, of course, we always did.

One evening we heard Mum's familiar cry through the letter-box. Dad wanted us back home and she had been sent to collect us. There was no greeting, no hello kiss, just a hasty 'Come on, you three. Get your coats on.' She seemed even more agitated and nervous than usual. Auntie protested that she was about to put us to bed, but it did no good. If Dad had ordered us home, we had to go. Mum asked Auntie for money, but Auntie had no more than two pounds to give her and that only increased Mum's agitation. She knew it would not be enough and that she would be in for a hiding again. The three of us kissed Auntie goodbye and trailed silently behind Mum to the bus-stop, wondering what was in store for us. On the bus we stared silently out of the windows.

At home, we were told we were going on an outing the next day and sent straight to bed. This was bad news. Every now and then Dad would decide we were going out somewhere, but these day trips were no fun – they were miserable occasions. He would usually take us to Southend and strut about all day, playing the doting family man, with Mum on his arm and us following behind. We dreaded these outings because they were all about Dad and what he wanted, and we were just pawns in the exercise. They were his excuse to parade up and down and stuff himself with fish and chips and ice cream. He had no interest at all in what we might like and, although we got treated too, the food stuck in our throats because we knew there would be a heavy price to pay.

Dad ran outings like a dictator, and because of this even fairground rides on the pier, which in other circumstances we might have enjoyed, became ordeals. He did not come on the rides with us or watch us as we went round. We were just plonked on them and left to get on with it. At the end there was no 'Did you enjoy it?' or hug – we were just ordered on to the next ride no matter whether we wanted to go on it or not. Worst of all was the dread of knowing that the effort of putting on a civilised face all day would put Dad into an even more foul mood than usual when we got home, and we would be the butt of it. Invariably he would have spent most of the week's benefits on the outing, and then we would be blamed because there was no money left.

That night we lay in bed listening to Dad shouting and raging at Mum. He was furious that she had not managed to squeeze more than two pounds from 'the old bag'. He ordered her out of the house and told her not to come back until she had some more money. It was the early hours before I heard her come in.

When we got up Mum packed some sandwiches and a thermos in a carrier bag – one of the few benefits of an outing was that we did get some food – and we set off, though not for our usual Southend bus. The one we were told to get on was going in the opposite direction. We did not dare ask where we were going, but just sat still and waited. Half an hour later we switched to another bus, a green one, which headed out of the city towards green fields and open spaces.

On top of the bus Kim was sitting next to Mum. Laurence, who by this time had developed a stammer and was very shy, was next to an old man who was chatting to him in a friendly way. I wished I could sit with Laurence, near Mum at the back of the bus, but Dad had glared at me and made it quite clear that I was supposed to sit next to him at the front. I tried to leave a gap between us, but he pulled me closer to him and, after a last drag, threw his cigarette butt on the floor and ground it under his foot. I could smell his tobacco-laden breath as he leaned towards me and began to whisper,

'You're a pretty little thing, y'know, Jenny. You're a big girl now, aren't you?'

I tried to smile back at him, but my stomach was turning over with fear. Why was he saying these things? A moment later he put his hand on my leg and moved it up under my dress, squeezing and pinching my thigh. I tried to move away, but before I could do so his arm was around me, pinning me tightly to him, while the other was thrust inside my knickers. My face was buried under his arm and I could smell his stale sweat. I felt sick and my tongue felt swollen in my mouth. He had forced my legs apart and his large, rough fingers were probing me.

What did he want? Why was Dad doing this? I could not understand it and I prayed for him to stop. He was whispering in my ear again, telling me to open my legs and promising that if I did what he wanted it would give me a nice feeling. But it wasn't nice – he was hurting me and I wanted him to stop. I could not hold back the hot tears of shame and confusion, though I dared not make a sound.

Then suddenly he stopped, grinning his yellow, tombstone grin at me. 'We've got to get off the bus now. That was nice, wasn't it, Jenny? You can have lots more of that later.' He winked at me and I stared at him, shocked. Did he think I had liked it? Was he really going to do it again? I pulled my dress back into place and followed him off the bus. I suddenly needed to wee, urgently. Mum glanced at my red, tear-stained face but said nothing, and I pressed my legs together to stop myself wetting my knickers.

When we got off the bus we were in a country lane and there was not a soul or a house in sight. It was a beautiful sunny day and we stood under the shade of a tree while Dad got out a map and looked at it. Then he ordered us to follow him up a tree-lined lane. We could hear faint voices in the distance, and as we rounded a bend we saw a high fence with a huge iron gate set into it. Beyond the gate was a sign saying 'Admissions' with an arrow underneath it. We children were told to wait while Mum and Dad went to a small, cabin-like building inside the gate. Suddenly a man came in sight, carrying a hosepipe spurting water. We stared open-mouthed. The man was stark naked and, even more oddly, did not even seem to realise it. Kim began to giggle, but the man looked annoyed and Laurence dug her in the ribs.

A few minutes later Dad strode towards us, looking like thunder. Mum followed him, stumbling along with the carrier bags. He frogmarched us back down the lane to the tree where we had stopped earlier and then began storming at Mum. Incredibly, Dad had tried to take us to a nudist camp for the day. Perhaps to him it was an opportunity to humiliate and confuse us, while he could enjoy parading around without his clothes and looking at nude women for the day. Of course, I did not understand at the time what this strange place with the naked man was, and it only made sense much later. Dad's plan had been thwarted because we had not got enough money to get in, and as far as he was concerned it was Mum's fault. He pushed her against the tree, so that she dropped the carrier bag and the contents spilled out all over the road. We rushed to pick the things up and luckily, before he could shove her again, the bus arrived and we all climbed on. The journey home took a long time, but Dad, furious that his plan had not worked, sat on his own chain-smoking and I was grateful to be able to sit at the back with the others.

Once home we had the packed lunch we had never had a chance to eat served up as our tea, and were sent to bed early. I could not sleep, and lay awake for what seemed like ages. Then I heard the heavy tread of Dad's step on the stairs.

I pulled the blankets up to my neck and pretended to be asleep, but I heard our door open and felt his hot breath as he bent over me. Terrified, I prayed he would go away, but he knelt down beside my bed and slipped his hands under the covers. I could see his lips, wet and glistening, as he promised to finish off what he had started on the bus.

He told me to take off my knickers and open my legs and he forced his fingers inside me, at the same time covering my mouth with his and forcing his tongue in between my teeth. By this time he had removed one of his hands and unzipped his trousers. Suddenly he began to jerk backwards and forwards, making strange sounds and pushing his fingers harder into me. Then suddenly he shuddered and stopped, collapsing and burying his face in my chest. A minute later he got up, did his trousers up, told me to put my knickers back on and promised me that I could look forward to plenty more nights like this.

When he had left I held myself close and cried. I could not understand why Dad wanted to hurt me like this. And he was going to do it again – he had said so. I looked across at Kim in the next bed. Her eyes were wide open. Had she seen what Dad had done? Suddenly I realised I had wet my bed. I did not think of telling Mum or Dad. He would have beaten me, and she would not have done anything at all. Changing the sheets or cleaning me up would not have occurred to her either, nor would comforting me or wondering why I had done it. As always, I knew I had to deal with it on my own. Some time later I fell asleep, sore, bewildered, frightened and soaked in urine.

Our surroundings were soon as appalling as the way we were treated. Within months of moving in, our new home was almost as much of a tip as the old one had been. The lovely new kitchen had become grease-spattered and filthy, with the cooker black and coated in burned and spilled food. The larder was always empty and the little fridge stank of mould. The sinks and bath had become stained and dirty, and the new carpet we had loved to feel under our bare feet was by now gritty and thick with dirt. The lovely new coal bunker was almost always empty. We would hear the coalman arriving at the flats, but he usually passed our door without delivering because we had not paid him for weeks. The windows were grimy and the furniture – even the few new bits – stained and grubby. The lovely cream walls in the living room were turning brown and the net curtains were yellow with nicotine. Overflowing ashtrays were everywhere and the air stank of stale fags and body odour.

It was the same story in the bedrooms. The sheets were hardly ever changed. Whenever one of us wet the bed we just lay in it until it dried and then went to bed in the same stinking sheets the next night, and the next, and the next. . . . Bedbugs became a real problem. I used to lie in bed, feeling little creatures crawling all over me, until I could stand it no more and threw back the covers in time to see them scuttle away. We were covered in bites, but no one took the least interest and so we learned to put up with them. Headlice were the same. We all got lice, as did many kids round about, but Mum never washed or combed ours out. We had so many that they would be crawling on our pillows when we got up in the morning.

But the worst place in the house was the toilet. There was never any toilet paper. At best there would be a scrap of newspaper, but sometimes not even that, and excrement was smeared all over the once pretty blue walls – though no one ever admitted to putting it there. Perhaps it was us children, but then what choice did we have when there was no paper? The slimy floor was swarming with hundreds of silverfish and other creepy-crawlies and the smell was vile. The toilet itself was heavily stained and disgusting. Despite all this, it seemed to be one of Dad's favourite places. After settling himself down he would call us all for what he termed a 'conference call' but was actually another opportunity to humiliate and frighten us. He would make us stand in front of him while he performed, meanwhile talking about the plans he had for some event or outing. Dad was a dreamer and always had big ideas of how things would change, or of grand events he would organise. We would stand there, too scared to move or even to look at each other, gagging on the terrible smell, until eventually he finished and told us we could go.

Our clothes were always dirty and our underwear stained. The only time we were cleaned up and de-loused was when we went to Auntie's. She would tut-tut away as she scrubbed us and put us into fresh clothes while she boiled our old ones with bicarbonate of soda in a big pan over her small stove. Auntie had taught us that it was important to be clean, so we three children tried our best at home. Sometimes we could earn a few pennies by taking other people's laundry to the bagwash shop, and we would sneak a few of our own things in with theirs. Laurence tried to make his room nice by cutting out pictures from magazines and sticking them on the walls, and Kim and I would do our best to tidy up and clean ourselves. But it was a hopeless task. With no soap, shampoo, flannels or toothbrushes we had no chance of improving things and there was little we could do but wait for our next visit to Auntie, which might be days, weeks or months away.

The flat was not just filthy, it was often freezing too. Dad never put money in the electric or gas meters, so we often had no heat and no light. We would have to manage with a couple of candles and cold food. Once Dad found a way to get the lock off the gas meter, but of course the gas company found out and when the man called we all had to be quiet and pretend we were out.

Once in a while Dad would decide to 'do up' one of the rooms. He would spend most of the week's benefit money on paint and make a big thing of announcing to anyone who would listen that he was 'decorating the place'. He once painted the kitchen tangerine and invited all the neighbours in to see it when he had finished. But within weeks it was filthy again, the gleaming paint covered with spatters of grease and fat, dirty fingerprints, splashes of food and layers of dust and dirt.

Meanwhile Dad's night-time visits to me had become a regular event. Every night I would lie in bed, my stomach clenched with fear, listening for his tread on the stairs. Even on the nights when he did not come into my room I could not relax – I would lie, tense and rigid, dreading the door opening and his face leering over me. But all too often he did come in, and he became quickly more demanding. If I tried to refuse he would get angry, and I soon learned that it would be over more quickly if I just submitted to what he wanted.

When he loomed over me in the night I could see the spit on his mouth glistening as his face came towards mine. His bristly face was covered in small shaving cuts and his rough hands, with their long, grimy nails, were stained orange from nicotine. His body was even worse. As time went on he got more adventurous and he would try to force me to take his penis into my mouth, grabbing me by my hair and forcing my head down as he undid his flies. 'Suck it,' he'd say. 'It tastes just like a lollipop.' His huge erection terrified me and the stench of his genitals made me retch.

One night he stripped off his trousers, which terrified me even more because until then he had just unzipped them and pulled his penis out. What was he going to do? I could see scabs and ulcers down the front of his legs, caused by burns when he had sat too close to the fire, and he was covered in splayed red lines from burst varicose veins. As he thrust his penis towards my mouth and pushed his coarse fingers inside me he muttered, 'This is special, between you and me, Jenny, so don't tell anyone.' Then he put his mouth over my private parts, and as he became more excited he bit and squeezed the tender skin there and on the tops of my thighs. It was so painful I had to struggle hard not to scream. I tried not to think about what was happening. I looked at the chink of light coming in at the window and concentrated on that, telling myself, 'It will be over soon . . . it will be over soon.' I was so tense that I held my breath and only let it out when he had finished.

Kim knew something bad was going on, but at only three years old she did not understand why Dad was in our room or why I was crying. She had the sense to pretend to be asleep, though, until he had left and she heard me sobbing quietly to myself. Then she put out a hand to me and whispered, 'It's all right, Jenny. He's gone away.' However, it was not long before Dad decided Kim was old enough to play his games too. I was his favourite – he preferred my blonde hair and blue eyes to Kim's dark looks. But that did not stop him. Kim was hauled into his bed for early morning 'cuddles' too, and I knew it would only be a matter of time before he went further.

5

On Our Own

School, like pre-school, came as a welcome relief from the miseries of home. All three of us in our time went to Burbage Primary, housed in an austere Victorian building a few streets away from home. Although there were plenty of nasty kids ready to give me a hard time there were also kids in the same boat as me, ready to make friends. The teachers were strict, but not unkind. We were in awe of them and would not have dreamed of arguing or being cheeky. We sat in our classroom on little wooden chairs at little wooden desks and did as we were told.

Learning was a serious business in those days. There was hardly ever any chatter or noise in our classroom. Mostly we had our lessons in silence, watching the teacher as she stood in front of her big blackboard and only speaking if we were spoken to. The classroom was not brightly decorated, like classrooms today, and there were no cheerful posters on the walls or displays we had made. We had pens, paper and paint pots, and that was about all.

For assembly we would file in lines into the large hall, where the teachers sat on wooden chairs on the platform and we all sat cross-legged on the floor. The headmaster, Mr Donohue, knew each one of us by name. He would stand in the middle of the platform, telling us about plans for the day while his little black poodle Cherry sat patiently at his feet. She went everywhere with him, and the two were a familiar sight around school. Mrs Rigden, who wore her hair in a tight bun and had glasses perched on the end of her nose, would play the piano while we all sang a hymn, followed by the Lord's Prayer. Another of the teachers, Miss Tinline, had a voluptuous figure like film star Jayne Mansfield and was known by all the kids as 'Titsy Tinline'. Thank goodness she never heard her nickname – she was a very strict teacher who brooked no nonsense.

Mostly school was not too bad – I was fairly bright and could keep up without a problem. The worst time for us very poor kids was PE. I hated it. We would have to strip down to our vests and knickers, and mine were always filthy and usually falling to bits as well. Another girl, called Miriam Ridsdale, was very like me: we were the ones with untidy hair and dirty faces, scruffy little kids in tatty clothes and scuffed shoes, who looked as though they had never had a wash. Miriam was one of nine kids and one day, when we were told to get ready for PE, she turned out to be wearing her brother's vest and her mum's knickers. She was a skinny little thing – we used to call her 'Skinny Minnie' – and her mum's knickers fell almost to her knees. She had to hold them up with both hands, her face burning with shame, as we walked down the corridor to the assembly hall where we did PE when it rained. Miriam and I often sat next to one another. She lived at the other end of Hoxton Market from us and I would sometimes see her there looking around for the left-over fruit and veg, just like us. Every day at break time we were given small bottles of milk. We all had to sit up straight with our arms folded while they were handed out. Those of us who needed it most, like Miriam and me, were always given our milk first – I suppose we stuck out like sore thumbs.

I was happy to play with anyone, but the smart kids turned their noses up at us and called us names. I envied girls like Julie Welton and Mary-Ann Merton, who had shiny, clean hair and beautiful clothes. They would not have dreamed of playing with us grubby kids. One day Mary-Ann was eating a fizzy sweet when she swallowed it whole and began to choke. She ran to the water fountain to get a drink, but the sweet would not budge. So I thumped her hard on the back and the sweet got dislodged. Mary-Ann said, 'Thanks, Ponting' and was nice to me for the rest of the day, but it was only a temporary respite – next day she was calling me names again.

There was another girl called Betty Upthon who was a real tough cookie and loved to pick on me. She was queen of the classroom and everyone was scared of her, but she specialised in terrorising the poorest kids. She would tell me she was going to beat me up after school, and there would be nothing I could do but wait for it to happen. Several times she beat hell out of me and I arrived home with a split lip or black eye. No one at home was bothered, so I just bathed the injury in some water and swore revenge.

School dinners were terrible – even those of us who were hungry and needed a hot meal could not stand them. The dinner hall was the domain of Mrs White, a tall, thin woman with a pointed nose and thin lips who reminded us of a witch and was really scary. She would stand in the middle of the hall shouting, 'Up the middle and round!' as we filed in and took our places on little benches either side of the trestle tables. We had to eat everything on our plates, so when it was a really horrible meal we would beg for small portions. The worst was meat pie, mash and cabbage. The pie would be full of gristle and tough, chewy bits, the potato dry and lumpy and the cabbage watery. Sometimes, when I just could not get it down, I would be left in the dinner hall with a handful of other children, staring at the congealing food on our plates and wishing we could be outside playing. Mrs White stood over us, arms folded and lips pursed, until we had eaten everything, no matter how long it took. As a result we became adept at getting rid of our food. We would take a scrap of paper to wrap the nastiest bits in and pop it in our pockets. If there was no paper handy we would hoard the stuff in our mouths like hamsters and hold it there till we got outside and could spit it out.

Playtimes were great. We chanted playground songs while we played with rubber balls, or we played Scoobydoo, a game which involved hundreds of rubber bands joined together. Marbles we played on the old drains, using a motley collection of marbles we had managed to put together.

Every day when we came out of school an ice-cream van was waiting there. There was also a man who had a bike with a huge basket on the front who would call out, 'Toffee apples, nice, juicy toffee apples.' It was tuppence for a single and threepence for a double, but I hardly ever had the money to buy either a toffee apple or an ice-cream. We found a new way to make money, though, which occasionally paid for one of the delicious sticky-sweet toffee apples. We would rummage through the local rubbish tips and bins to find old clothes and rags, and once we had a big bag of them we could take it to a shop at the end of Hoxton

Market. It was a musty, dirty place where a man would weigh the clothes on a big set of scales and give up a couple of pennies for them. He would often invite me into the back room when I went there, but he had the same look on his face as Dad did when he was about to force me to do horrible things with him, and I always hurried away telling him I had to get home.

I did not miss school often, as it was much better than being at home. There were times when one or other of us had no option, though, because Dad had beaten us black and blue and he did not want the teachers asking questions about our injuries. And more than once I had to stay away because I had no shoes. The only shoes we had were provided by the state. A voucher was sent to our parents, which had to be taken to Curtess's shoe shop, on the corner of Hoxton Market. The shoes there were cheap and nasty and very old-fashioned, but we had to take what we got and no fuss was allowed. When Mum took me there and the stern assistant tried some shoes on me I would say they fitted even if they did not, because I was scared that otherwise I would get no shoes at all. At least we got new shoes, though. Mum had tiny feet, and once my feet had grown as big as hers she used to wear my old shoes when I had outgrown them.

Sometimes the new voucher did not arrive before the shoes wore out, or our feet outgrew them to the point where we could not wear them any more. Then we had no choice but to stay at home until the voucher arrived. Once when this had happened, and I got back to school wearing my hideous new shoes, the teacher asked me why I had been away. Mum would not have written any notes to explain even if she could have, so I told the truth and said, 'Please, miss, I had no shoes.' The rest of the class gasped – all except for a girl called Maggie Lumsden. She understood, because she had had to miss school waiting for new shoes too.

On school mornings we got up very early in order to get our chores done. Dad had ordered us to clear out the grate in the living room every morning and set a new fire. We would go downstairs, barefoot and shivering in our vests and knickers. If it was really cold we could see our own breath. We would scrape out the old ashes and burned bits of coal on to newspaper and bundle that up before laying and lighting a new fire. After we had got the fire going we would go through to the kitchen, fill the kettle and put it on the hob – listening to the usual routine which had already begun. Dad would be laying into Mum, cursing her and hitting her as she whimpered at him to stop or screamed in pain. This would be followed, as ever, by the panting, gasping noises of sex.

Our next job was to take a cup of tea up to Dad. Kim and I both dreaded this errand and tried to get out of it, but inevitably one of us would have to take it. The stench of the bedroom always made us gag and we tried to get out as fast as possible, but most days he would order whichever one of us had taken the tea into the bed with him. He did not bother trying to coax us, it was: 'Get in this bed, you little cunt' and we would have to do as he said and submit to his horrible, shameful games. I never associated these 'games' with the 'sex' which by now we vaguely knew went on between Mum and Dad. It was only later that the penny dropped and I realised he was trying to do to Kim and me what he did to Mum. After he had let us go we had to carry on getting ourselves ready for school as though nothing had happened. I used to go into the bathroom and splash water on my face, trying to wash away the tears and the shame and the anger.

Breakfast was, as always, uncertain. Sometimes, if we were lucky, there might be some cereal. But if there was, there would be no milk. And if there was milk, there would be no cereal. We got one box of cereal a week, and the boxes often had free gifts in them. Trolls were the big thing then, and the three of us would fight over these ugly little plastic creatures with their long purple or green hair as though they were treasured prizes. It mattered little who won, though, because Dad would usually make up some excuse to take the little objects away from us. By the time breakfast was over and we were dressed it was a relief to get out of the house and go to school. Being the grubby, smelly, bullied kids at school had to be better than spending another minute with Dad.

On weekends and holidays, of course, we were still turfed out of the house after breakfast and ordered not to come home until evening. One day I went over to the swing park by the museum where a group of kids were pretending to put on a play. Asked to join in, I grabbed the chance. As an escaped convict I had to say a few lines and then run from the stage and jump on to the stone seats at the front. I missed, and my shin crunched on the edge of the stone. A huge gap appeared, pouring with blood. I tried to stem the flow, worried that my sock would be covered in it, but it was hopeless and blood continued to pour down my leg. It was obvious that the wound needed stitches but, back home, Mum and Dad had no interest in taking me to hospital. I had to clean it up myself, and it was a neighbour who eventually got me a dressing to put over it. It was horribly painful, but there was no sympathy or support – I just had to get on with things.

Soon after the accident Dad came into my room as usual. I was feeling a little braver that night, and when he pulled the blanket off me and told me to get my knickers off I said no. For a moment we were both surprised by my boldness. But it didn't take Dad long to recover. He demanded that I do as I was told, and when I still hesitated he put his hand on my injured shin and pressed on the wound so hard that blood seeped through the dressing. It hurt so much that my face screwed up and I begged him to stop, but he laughed and told me he would stop when I did as I was told. Sobbing with pain, I had to promise to be a 'good girl' and take off my knickers. That night he was rougher than ever, biting me and jamming his rough fingers inside me over and over again. It was as though the sight of me in pain gave him some kind of awful pleasure.

The next day I felt bruised and sore all over. The wound on my leg was throbbing and I could barely limp. It took a long, long time to heal, and when it finally did I ended up with a round hole in my shin that is still there today.

One of our favourite places to play was the disused factory down the road, which the kids all called the Secret F. The factory, derelict for years, was crumbling and dangerous and we were all banned from playing there. That did nothing to stop us, though: we loved it – to us it could be a pirate ship, a castle or an outlaw's hideaway. It was on three floors, but only part of the top floor remained and the other two were accessible via a crumbling staircase whose missing steps we had filled in with lumps of wood and concrete. The basement was flooded with stagnant water and we made stepping stones so that we could get across it to the stairs. It was an adventure playground that we all loved, but how dozens of us played in the Secret F day after day without the whole place collapsing on us I shall never know. From time to time one of us did get hurt, but we were sworn to secrecy and so we never told an adult how the accident had happened. Next to the Secret F was a piece of waste ground that had become overgrown with weeds and shrubs. We called this the Jungle and we spent many happy hours there, collecting caterpillars and other bugs in buckets and jars.

A lot of the kids who lived around us were the same ones who had been our neighbours and taunted us in Cherbury Street. Things were not much better in Monteagle Court. We were still bottom in the pecking order, still the smelly Pontings who looked like ragamuffins. But we hung around the other kids so much that some of them eventually let us join in their games and we won a kind of acceptance.

Laurence was less interested in being part of the crowd than Kim and I. We wanted to belong, but he was always happy spending time on his own. Laurence was a bright boy and from his early years it was clear that he was going to be a high flyer and take a different path. At home Dad was more interested in us girls because he could use us for sex, so although Laurence still got his share of beatings he had more opportunity than we did to stay out of Dad's way. He also had his own room, where he would spend hours making models or reading anything he could get his hands on.

Laurence was the first of us to work out ways of deflecting Dad when trouble was brewing. He would say, 'Let's have a game of chess, Dad', and sometimes it worked – but only if he let Dad win. Laurence was really good at chess, but he had to pretend otherwise. Dad liked games, but only because they gave him an opportunity to beat everyone else. He would make us play chess and Monopoly with him whether we wanted to or not. In Monopoly he always had to be the banker and we always had to make sure he won. If not he would bring his hand up under the board, sending it flying off the table and throwing all the pieces on to the floor. We kids would scrabble about for the little green houses and red hotels, while Dad stormed and raged at us. Not surprisingly, none of us has ever been able to stand Monopoly since.

Kim and I liked to sit on the window-sill of our shared bedroom and watch a family who lived in a flat across the road. In the evening, when they had put the lights on but not yet drawn their curtains, we caught a glimpse of their family life as they moved around. We would see the kids running freely from room to room, and later the mum or dad carried them into the room wrapped in big towels after their bath. We would watch them being tickled and played with and getting into their pyjamas, and saw their parents laughing with them. Kim would laugh too, when she watched this, and then we would act it out. I would be the mum, tickling Kim and playing with her and pretending to wrap her in a towel. Kim loved it – it was the closest either of us ever got to warmth and affection.

We longed to have a pet, but Dad would hear nothing of it. Then one day Kim found a little black mongrel dog wandering in the street. He was the sweetest creature, who cocked his head to one side and looked at us with absolute trust in his eyes, and we instantly decided to adopt him. We called him Buster, tied a piece of string round his neck as a lead and, when Dad was not looking, hid him in our bedroom. This was a wildly reckless move on our part, but Buster did his best to help. He was incredibly docile and well behaved, as though he understood what he had to do, and he submitted to being shoved under the bed or hidden under a blanket with good-natured resignation. Buster, with his stumpy little tail, floppy ears and quirky expression, became very special to all three of us. For the first time in our lives we could express love without being shunned or rejected. We showered him with hugs, strokes and cuddles and he lapped it all up, wagging his tail manically and licking our noses in appreciation.

We managed to keep him hidden for just three days before Dad went into our room and spotted him slipping out from under the bed. Dad went mad. He shouted to us to come upstairs and raged, throwing Buster across the room, kicking him and shrieking at the top of his voice. All three of us hung on to Dad's arms, crying and pleading, trying to stop him hurting Buster. We could not bear seeing our beloved dog whimpering in pain and cowering against the wall; at that moment I think any one of us kids would have killed Dad if we could. When he tired of shouting and lashing out he ordered us to get rid of Buster. Knowing that if we did not do so Dad would probably kill him, we promised to give him away and led him out of the house.

On the ground at the back of the flats we sat and hugged Buster, who was still whimpering and trembling violently from the kicking Dad had given him. Kim and I were both crying and Laurence was close to tears. 'I love him,' Kim sobbed. 'I don't want to give him away.'

What could we do? We had no one to give Buster to, and in any case none of us could bear the thought of letting him go. With courage born of desperation, we hatched a plan. We would wait until dark and then smuggle Buster back inside, keep him hidden for the night and then smuggle him back out before Dad got up. Amazingly, it worked. We got him out by lowering him from our window in a cardboard box on the end of a piece of string. One of us would let it down while another stood under the window and caught it. Then we would pull him back up the same way at night. Buster did his bit by keeping quiet; he never barked or whined once during the nights, and after two weeks Dad still had not suspected a thing.

Sadly, Buster's perfect behaviour did not extend to daylight hours, and one day when Kim and I were walking him he bit a nun, who stormed round to our house to complain. When he realised we still had the dog Dad grabbed Buster and took him straight down to Brick Lane Market, where he sold him for a few pennies before coming home and giving us a thrashing which left us badly bruised for several days.

The loss was awful. We cried for Buster long after our bruises had healed, and Kim and I kept his empty cardboard box in our room for six months. We missed him terribly and used to lie in bed at night and tell each other Buster stories, about the heroic little dog who came to save three children from a monster.

A few months later someone gave us a hamster. I can't remember why – probably because they could not afford to look after it. For some reason of his own, Dad let us keep it. But we had no food to give it, so it started chewing the living room curtains and, not surprisingly, we soon found it dead.

Our only other foray into the world of pets was when Dad arrived home from the market one day with two budgies in a cage. It was typical of him to buy something like that on a whim. The budgies were called Peter and Paul, after the two little birds in the nursery rhyme. Peter was light blue and Paul was dark blue. Dad would let them out and they would fly around the living room, much to our delight. Of course, their cage soon became filthy and caked in excrement because no one ever cleaned it out. One day I spotted a swelling over Peter's eye. I was terribly worried, but Dad would not have dreamed of taking the bird to the vet so there was nothing I could do. A couple of mornings later I got up and Peter was gone. Dad would not say where, just, 'You'd better get used to it, because the other one'll be gone soon.' A few days later Paul was absent too. We were dreadfully upset, but Dad was not about to give us an explanation. He told us to clean out the cage and sell it. We reckoned he had got bored with the novelty and wrung both their necks.

We still spent a lot of our time trying to solve our biggest problem – hunger. We would go home and ask Mum when dinner was going to be ready, and half the time she would say, 'I don't know – your father's got no fucking money,' and that would be it. So a lot of the time we had to find food for ourselves, and we became brilliant foragers. If we were lucky enough to find a bottle and get the deposit back from the off-licence it would buy us a penny portion of batter from the fish and chip shop. The proprietor would scoop up all the bits of batter that had fallen off the fish and put them in a bag for us. Another treat from the chip shop was a small loaf, hollowed out and filled with chips. Or we would go to the blue shop and buy a bag of crisps – much more filling than sweets.

However, there were not that many bottles to be found, and we had quickly discovered other ways to make some money. We would offer to wash cars for those people lucky enough to have one, to run errands, to take washing to the bagwash shop or to look after toddlers for harassed mothers. We would take the little ones over to the Jungle and play games with them, or make daisy chains for hours on end. The sixpence we were paid at the end of the day felt like riches and meant that all three of us could eat that night.

But there were plenty of times when there was no food and no money and we kids were desperate. On those days, like other kids from poor families, we would go over to Hoxton Market at the end of the day, when the traders and stall-holders were packing up, and pick through the piles of rotten fruit and veg left behind for the dustmen. Anything remotely edible would be grabbed and eaten. Mostly we found apples, carrots and spuds, but now and then we would find an orange and we would be on cloud nine.

Although there was often no dinner at home, Mum would try to buy something each week to put aside for Christmas. Dad had a big thing about Christmas, so a tin of strawberries or a packet of custard powder would go into the kitchen cupboard with strict orders that we were not to touch it. But we were so hungry that we would wait until our parents were asleep and then take one of the tins back upstairs. Having hidden a tin-opener and some spoons there earlier we would open the tin and sit on the bed, eating the fruit as fast as we could in case Dad woke up. We would take turns tipping the juice into our mouths, and when we had finished we would hide the spoons and the opener again until we could sneak them downstairs. The tin would be chucked out of the window on to the open patch at the back of the flats. Amazingly, Mum and Dad never guessed. Neither of them ever bothered to check the number of items in the cupboard, and we were careful to take things from the back so that it did not look disturbed. After a couple of years there were empty tins and packets all over that patch of ground, ample evidence of our guilt, but hilariously, and thankfully for us, our parents never put two and two together. And anyway, just how 'guilty' were three little kids of primary school age whose Mum and Dad were happy to let them starve?

6

The Tyrant

Dad loved to play the big man. He was really taken by the idea of people looking up to him and being impressed. Not content with pretending he had been a brave soldier wounded in action, he was always looking for ways to show off to the neighbours. Of course, most of them loathed and despised him. We would see the looks they gave him and hear their comments: 'Bloody idiot. Who does he think he is?', 'Prat', 'Nasty bully' and so on, but they did not say it to his face and he never seemed to realise – or perhaps he just did not care.

Bonfire night was one of his favourite occasions. He would spend two weeks' benefits and send us to invite all the neighbours to 'the Pontings' fireworks show'. Everyone came because a free fireworks show was not to be passed up, whatever they thought of him. Dad would make a big thing of organising the display and setting the fireworks off, and everyone would ooh and aah at the effects. We watched him showing off and knew we would all pay for it. And we did. For the next two weeks there was barely anything to eat because Dad had spent all the food money on fireworks.

Behind the closed door of our flat Dad considered himself king. He was the undisputed ruler who had to be obeyed and who could do anything he pleased – a mini-tyrant. His favourite saying was 'This is my fucking castle, my word is law.' As far as he was concerned, the rest of us were just there for him to order about. I do not think he felt any genuine affection for any of us – he certainly never showed any.

We were always wary and cautious around him, knowing that the next attack could come out of the blue at any time. Sometimes he would swipe at one of us with his hand, knocking us off our feet, with no warning and for no reason at all. As always, he would be provoked to violence by the tiniest thing: treading on some small object on the floor, a spot of grease on his newspaper, running out of cigarettes, not getting a cup of tea fast enough . . . the list was endless.

Dad very rarely left the house, and seemed almost afraid of the world outside his little castle. Apart from his firework displays and the odd time he got the chance to show off to the neighbours, virtually the only time he went out was when he had to visit the social security offices for an interview concerning his benefits. He would take one of us with him, saying it was in case he suffered one of his 'blackouts' – which he invariably did as soon as the officials started asking him awkward questions.

Mostly Dad sent us children to carry out all his errands, but this was a dangerous business. If we failed to come back with exactly what he wanted, we got a beating. It mattered not that the shop was shut, or that he had not given us enough money – we still suffered for it. Sometimes when he was about to attack us we would see what was coming and run for the door. He would stick out a foot to stop us and we would run around the room trying to escape, while he chased after us raining blows. When he made us strip as a punishment, which he did often, it was especially hard for Laurence who was an intensely private boy with a fierce sense of justice. Dad's punishments were torture to him. He was a skinny little boy, a bag of bones, and he would stand with his hands over his private parts, red-faced with anger and shame, struggling to hold back his tears.

Although Mum just turned a blind eye to the sexual abuse, she sometimes tried to intervene to prevent violence. If she could see that Dad was about to lose it she would grab us, muttering, 'Get the fuck out – I'll deal with it.' She would push us out of the front door, knowing that the full force of his fury and venom would be taken out on her. He would throw kettles, irons, pots and bottles at her, often hitting her and leaving her badly cut or bruised. If he did not like his food he would hurl his full plate at her, smashing the plate and spattering food all over her and around the room. Mum liked to try out home perm and colouring kits. But if her style was not to Dad's liking she would get a beating. 'Wash yer fucking hair, yer soppy fucker, and get rid of those curls!' he would yell while laying into her. It happened all too often.

One night Kim woke me up in alarm and cried out, 'Jenny, Mum's being killed.' I tried to get her to stay in our room, but she ran into our parents' room and I followed. Laurence had woken up too, and he ran through after us. Our parents were both naked and Mum was curled on the floor as Dad stood over her, raining down blows and screaming, 'You do as you're fucking told!' Kim accidentally stood on Mum's glasses and stopped in her tracks, Laurence and I behind her. There was blood all over the floor and we had no idea what part of Mum's body it had come from. We all started crying, and Kim ran to Mum and caught some of the blows from Dad. He picked her up by her vest and the skin on her chest. Kim was shouting, 'Leave her alone' and trying to kick him. He called her a 'fucking little mare' and then threw her on top of Laurence and me, shouting, 'Fuck off – this is between me and your mother.'

All three of us ended up on the floor sobbing. I yelled, 'Leave her alone – she's had enough. You're killing her.' He leaned over, his fist clenched as if he was going to hit us, snarling, 'Yer fucking mother won't do as she's told.' The veins were nearly popping through his throat, and the stench of his breath was revolting as he sprayed all three of our faces with his spit. We backed out of the room and the next sounds we heard were the two of them having sex. As always, Mum had given in to his demands. And, despite the awful things he did to Kim, Laurence and me, it was always Mum who got the worst of his violence.

Sometimes we were so frightened we would sneak out of the house and run up the road to the phone box and call the police. But when they arrived Dad would laugh and tell them it was all sorted, and they would go off again. Once I tried to stop one of them and tell him what was going on, but he told me to shut up and turned back to talk to Dad. Kids were simply not listened to in those days. Even though we were the ones who had called the police, they always ignored us as though we were completely irrelevant.

Occasionally Dad's brutality landed one of us kids in hospital, and once I had to go there even without him being the direct cause. When I was seven I was walking home from Nanny and Grand-ad Ponting's one day with a bag of broken biscuits Dad had sent me to collect, when I crossed the road without looking and got hit by a car. The driver ran over and knelt beside me saying, 'Oh, my God, are you all right?' I was confused and my arm was in pain, and all I could think of was that I knew Dad would be angry about the biscuits, which had spilled all over the road. I was frightened about what he would do. I said, 'I want my Mum' – I suppose it was an instinctive reaction, even though Mum had never really been there for me. Someone ran to get her and she took me to St Leonard's Hospital, where they put my broken arm in plaster. When we got home all Dad said was, 'You good-for-nothing little cunt.'

St Leonard's was a ten-minute walk away and we got to know it well. Mum was the one injured most often, and we would nurse her and clean her wounds and comfort her while she sobbed. When she was badly hurt the three of us would take her to the hospital and then wait, sitting on the hospital chairs swinging our legs, while they patched her up. Or we would play jumping games on the white painted lines in the courtyard outside until she came out.

Once Mum was cooking chips in a pan of hot dripping when she and Dad started an argument. Suddenly we heard her screaming and we ran in to see that the pan of hot fat had gone all over her legs. We could see it still bubbling on her skin. She said her arm had caught the pan handle, but we all knew that Dad had thrown it over her. She was in agony, but she still had to walk to hospital – there was no other way to get there. We went with her, while Dad, not in the least bothered, went back to his telly and fags. She was dreadfully burned. She came home with bandages all over both legs, and when they finally came off she was left with scars that were there for the rest of her life.

Sometimes Mum would try to escape from Dad when he was on the rampage. He would tell us she had run off and the three of us would trail around the neighbourhood looking for her, asking shop-keepers and neighbours if they had seen her and even going down to the hospital to see if she was there. We often found her in the blue shop; we would tell Dolly, 'We've come for our mum' and Dolly would take us through to the back, where Mum would be sitting with a compress on her battered face and a cup of tea. Dolly would usually give Mum some cigarettes for Dad, to 'shut him up' when she got home.

One of Dad's favourite pastimes was ordering things from catalogues. Mail order was just taking off in those days, and Dad had caught on to the fact that he could order all sorts of goods from his armchair and get them delivered to his door. He would send for every catalogue going and every time a new one arrived he would spend hours leafing through it, picking out the things he wanted. These would never be paid for, but when he was chased by the debtors and taken to court he always pleaded unemployment and was let off with a paltry fine. Although banned from ordering anything else from that source, he would simply move on to a new mail order company and a new catalogue.

Christmas was when Dad really came into his own with the catalogues: he would order decorations, hampers and gifts as though he were rolling in money. For us, it was the most bizarre time of year, for our smelly, grimy flat would be decorated from floor to ceiling. Dad would get a huge seven- or eight-foot-tall tree, haul it into the living room and trim it from top to bottom with tinsel and crackers. Some of the decorations he made himself. Dad had a talent for art and he spent hours sketching designs, measuring the living room and then drawing his designs to scale on graph paper. He would then ask us, at one of his toilet 'conferences', which design we preferred. The chosen one was then made up and hung around the living room. He was also good at calligraphy, and would write out place names in beautiful script for the Christmas dinner table.

Christmas may have been special to him, but it did not stop his violence. Once I accidentally broke a couple of the glass baubles for the tree. Dad erupted when he found the pieces, making all three of us strip naked and stand in front of him while he hit us and demanded to know who had broken them. I did not dare own up, I was too terrified of what he would do to me. We all stood there, shaking, while he tormented us, demanding to know who it had been. Laurence, wanting to protect me and Kim and realising that Dad was not going to stop until he had got a culprit, said he had done it. Dad ordered Kim and me upstairs and closed the door. From our room we could hear Laurence's screams as Dad vented his fury on him and I hid my head under a pillow, grateful to my brother for taking the blame but feeling terrible that he was suffering. I looked up to Laurence and admired him for his courage; this was not the only time he took the blame for us two girls.

Christmas was a time when Dad was even more likely to come up with a scheme for making money. Sometimes these were completely hare-brained, but every now and then he hit on something that worked. Making blackboards was one of his better ones. He bought the chalk board and the wood for easels and set up a mini-factory in the front room, with all of us helping. When he had enough black-boards he took them down to the market and sold them very fast for a handsome profit. This was something that, if he could have been bothered, Dad could actually have expanded to make into a decent business; but he was far too lazy. He made enough blackboards to bring in some extra money, and then gave up as soon as Christmas was over. He actually did it two or three Christmases running before he lost interest completely.

Our larder might have been pretty bare for the rest of the year, but at Christmas it was full to bursting. Not only would Mum have saved some food item every week, but Dad would order a couple of massive hampers full of things we had never heard of, like preserved fruit and cranberry sauce. Strangely, for such a violent man, he did not drink for the rest of the year and neither did Mum, but at Christmas bottles of sherry, whisky and gin would appear along with the preserves, pickles, hams, cakes and other fancy goods. For two days we would have enormous meals – a massive fry-up followed by a huge dinner. In fact there was more food around than we ever saw in total in our house during the rest of the year. But as soon as it was gone things went back to the way they were before.

It was the same with presents. Before Christmas we would all be invited to choose what we wanted from the catalogues. We had no toys at all for the rest of the year, but at Christmas Dad acted like Mr Bountiful, inviting us to pick four or five expensive gifts each. We would pore over pages of dolls, games, trains, cars and chemistry sets, hardly able to believe that they would really be ours, while Dad said, 'Go on, pick something else – have whatever you want.' On Christmas Eve we would go to bed full of excitement, waiting for Santa to leave our toys, and the next morning they would be laid out on our beds for us to open.

But, Dad being Dad, there was always a twist. When we opened our presents we would find that Dad had opened every game and toy and tried it out before we got it, as though he was a big kid who had to have everything first. We did not mind – we were just so happy to have some toys that we played with them nonstop for the next couple of days. But then the real blow would fall. Dad would order us to clean them all up, put them back in their wrappers and take them to Brick Lane to be sold. We would be heartbroken and say Santa had given them to us, but he would just laugh and say, 'There ain't no Santa, you little fuckers! Now hand 'em over.'

One year Kim had beautiful twin dollies and a twin pram to push them in. She loved them so much she sat and rocked them for hours, singing to them and taking them everywhere with her. When Dad said they had to go back she burst into tears and begged him to let her keep just one doll. But he told her to fuck off and grabbed the pram. Kim hung on to it and was dragged along behind it, sobbing, 'Please don't take it. Please don't take my babies.' Dad ignored her and yanked the pram away, and Kim was left with grazed legs and a broken heart.

The next year I got a beautiful doll whom I called

Diana. She was made of plaster, and had a painted face and brown curly hair. I loved her and took her everywhere with me. When the time came to sell our presents I could not bear to part with her, so I came up with a plan. I deliberately broke her arm off, but it hurt so much to do it that I kept telling her how sorry I was. I hugged her and put her in my bed. When Dad found out he was livid and I got a beating, but I did not care – Diana was still mine.

We were made to sell the toys ourselves. At dawn on the Sunday after Christmas we would get up and load them all into an old pram and a couple of battered holdalls. Then we would walk down Hoxton Market to Shoreditch High Street, across the junction of Hackney Road and Old Street and through to Brick Lane. It was an amazing place, packed with stalls selling everything under the sun and people looking for bargains. The first stalls sold animals. I would gaze at puppies and kittens, barking and mewling pathetically, and wish I could rescue them all. There were birds flapping and chirping, tropical fish, mice, hamsters, rats and even monkeys. All of them were packed into over-crowded cages and screeching at the tops of their voices. I hated seeing them.

We would push past them and carry on further down the street until we reached a narrow cobbled section beside a factory wall. This was where all the unofficial selling went on. People would bring anything they thought they could sell and lay it out on the pavement. At five in the morning it was already busy, but we always managed to find a spot and unload our goods. None of us liked it there. Odd people would come past and stare at us. There were plenty of immigrants and refugees, but what we did not know then was that it was an area haunted by prostitutes, and children were often 'sold' here to paedophiles. This was why we got stared at, and why Dad often left us to do the selling on our own – he knew we would attract customers.

Every now and then a kindly old lady would ask us, 'Are these your toys, dear?' but we were under strict instructions to smile and say 'no' so that people would not feel sorry for us and be put off buying. When we made a sale we felt relieved – we knew Dad would be pleased and that meant we would get a good meal. If we did well he would call into a shop on the way home to buy Bird's Eye frozen roast beef, potatoes and vegetables for our Sunday dinner. This was a real treat, because Mum, of course, could not cook to save her life. The alternative was Mum's idea of Sunday dinner – putting some mince in a baking tin with a few lumps of lard, a sprinkling of gravy powder and a bit of water and then sticking the whole thing in the oven for an hour or two. The result was tasteless muck, which would be accompanied by soggy cabbage and boiled potatoes.

As we got older we stopped being excited about Christmas. We knew that any toys we were given would have to go within a few days, so we tried not to let ourselves care about them. And although we liked the decorations they just covered over the grime in the flat, so that when they came down after Christmas the place looked more depressing than ever. Dad had destroyed any dreams we had about Santa Claus early on. And Christmas lost its last glimmer of magic for me the year he paid me a night visit on Christmas Eve to have a bit of 'fun', leaving me to look forward to Christmas Day bruised and in tears.

If Christmas was bad, New Year was often worse. Since we had usually just sold all our toys we children felt there was not much to celebrate. But Mum would say, 'Let's keep the kids up' and Dad would have a couple of sherries. Then he would decide he wanted to dance, and that's when things really started to go wrong. They would begin to jive, but if Mum put a foot wrong – and she always did – Dad would explode and throw her across the room. A huge row would follow, with Dad hitting Mum and the three of us cowering in a corner. After that we would be ordered to 'fucking get to bed' and we would hide under the bedclothes, listening to them fighting and wishing New Year's Eve would never come again.

One year, when I was six or seven, Dad woke up

in the middle of the night and ordered us downstairs. He had put all the lights, the telly and the
record player on and he was shouting, 'You want a
party? I'll give you a party. Dance, you little
fuckers, fucking dance.' Dazed, confused and still
half-asleep, we all tried to dance. We were wearing
the vests and knickers we slept in, so we were
freezing cold, but we tried to do what he wanted
because we knew that otherwise Mum would get a
worse beating – and he would start on us too.
Confused and frightened, we began jigging from
side to side to the blaring music. But Dad was not
satisfied. He bawled at us that we were not dancing
properly and hit us across our legs to make us jump
harder and faster. Smarting with pain and sobbing
with fear we tried to dance, until at last he tired of
torturing us and allowed us to crawl back to bed,
exhausted and bewildered.

The place we longed to be at Christmas and New
Year was with Auntie. But Dad would never allow
it. Auntie used to go to her sister Mary's and when
we were allowed to see her, usually some time after
New Year, she would celebrate with us. She would
make us a special meal and give us our presents –
almost always clothes, as she knew that any toys
would be taken away and sold.

Back in the safe haven of Auntie's flat we would
relax, the tensions and terrors of home temporarily
forgotten. Auntie would say to me, 'Has he touched

you, Jinnybelle? If there's anything going on you'll tell me, won't you?' But I couldn't tell her. Everything with Auntie was perfect: we were her pride and joy, and I did not want to change that. I did not want to feel tainted in her presence, or for our time with her to be spoilt. So I told her there was nothing going on. Then one day Kim let slip what Dad was doing to us. We could see the shock and horror on Auntie's face as she took in what Kim had said. For a few minutes she was silent. Then she said, 'Right.' She put our coats on and took us with her to Monteagle Court, where she left us outside and went in to see Dad. We waited, praying everything would be all right. We could hear Auntie and Dad shouting at each other, and she was saying, 'If you ever lay a finger on those children again. . . .' But Dad laughed at her and shouted, 'You tried to steal my fucking children! Get out, you old bag. You'll never see those fucking kids again.'

There was nothing Auntie could do. She left in tears, kissing us on her way out. We all began crying and ran after her, but Dad hauled us back inside and snarled, 'You can forget about her – you're not seeing your precious Auntie again.' If losing our toys was hard, the thought of losing Auntie was unimaginable. She was the sunshine in our lives, the person who truly loved us, who gave us cuddles, who sang us funny songs in her warbly voice and who provided an escape from the horrors of Monteagle Court. I felt as though my whole world was falling apart: to lose Auntie was to lose everything.

7

Babies

It was only a few weeks after the terrible confronta-
tion between Auntie and Dad that Mum gave us
some surprise news. She was going to have another
baby: a little brother or sister would be arriving in
the summer. Why she got pregnant again after a gap
of almost five years I shall never know. It was
certainly nothing to celebrate – even we children
knew that another baby would only mean another
mouth to feed and more work to do. Kim and I hoped
it would not be a girl. We knew that, if it was, she
would suffer at Dad's hands in the same way we had.

Mum was tired and run-down during her pregnancy and perhaps it was that, or maybe it was the
thought of the forthcoming extra mouth to feed,
which made Dad relent and allow us to go back to
Auntie's for a visit. Money was too tight for us to
afford the bus and we had to walk the whole way.
We were still too young to do it alone, so Mum,
now heavily pregnant, walked with us. It took an
hour and a half, but at least Auntie would always
give her the bus fare home.

We were thrilled to see Auntie and ran into her arms, where she hugged us as tightly as we hugged her. We had thought we would never see her again, and the fear of losing her made her seem even more precious. Although she was shocked and worried to see Mum pregnant again, she said very little in front of us. She scooped us up and took us off for our usual scrub-up and hot meal and then cuddled us in front of the telly, where we fought for the places on either side of her and clung to her arms as though we thought she might suddenly disappear.

It was the beginning of the summer holidays. By then I was seven, Laurence eight and Kim five. We spent a couple of happy weeks going for picnics and seeing the sights of London using Red Rover bus tickets. We would sit on top, heading for somewhere grand like Oxford Street or the City, enjoying the sights and scenes along the way. On Saturday we went to the morning children's show at the local cinema: we felt very grown up as we set off together with our ticket money and a little extra for a treat.

At night we slept so much better than at home. Free of nits, bedbugs and above all the fear of Dad's rough, probing fingers, I snuggled into Auntie's big, soft bed and slept like a baby. She would sing us to sleep, and we all had favourite songs. I loved 'Wait till the clouds roll by, Jenny, wait till the clouds roll by', which she sang over and over again to each of us in turn. Or she would sing her favourite hymn, 'There is a green hill far away'. Sometimes she chose comic songs and we would all join in and roll about the bed laughing. We loved 'My Uncle Joe's got a very red nose, he gets pinched wherever he goes', and

> I've got a sausage, a bonny, bonny sausage
> I put it in the oven for my tea
> I went down the cellar to fetch my umbrella
> And that sausage ran after me.

Our baby sister Carole was born on 21 August 1963. Laurence and I were still at Auntie's, but Kim was back at home. This was not unusual – one of Dad's power games was allowing only one or two of us to stay at Auntie's. Kim sat on the stairs with her hands over her ears, trying to blot out Mum's screams as Dad, with the help of Pam Williams from number eight, helped the baby into the world. I do not think they had planned a home birth – there was just not enough time to get Mum to hospital or even to get the midwife, who arrived in time to cut the cord and clean up. It gave Dad a wonderful opportunity to boast to the neighbours, telling anyone who would listen how he had saved the day by delivering his daughter in the nick of time, using a sanitary towel in each hand to bring her into the world.

A few days after the birth Mum arrived at Auntie's to collect Laurence and me, bringing our new sister with her. We peered into the pram at the beautiful baby with her blue eyes and downy blonde hair, and I wondered how we were going to manage with one more in the house. Carole was a big, healthy baby, which was amazing considering how slight Mum was and how dreadful her health must have been by then, given the beatings, endless smoking and lack of food. Unfortunately Mum put her down on Auntie's dressing table and the uric acid in the baby's wet nappy took the polish off the surface. There were heated words, not just about the damaged furniture but because Auntie found it hard to understand why Mum had produced another child when she could not look after the three she already had.

Dad had wanted a big christening for Carole, but, although they had done so for us three older children, this time Nanny and Grandad Ponting refused point-blank to pay for it or even to organise it. Like Auntie, they were stunned that their son and his wife had produced another child when they were unable to cope with the kids they already had. Our grandparents swore they would have nothing to do with any kind of celebration. But Dad was still determined to give a big party. He insisted on spending a couple of weeks' benefit money laying on food and drink for the gathering, which took place after Carole was 'topped and tailed' in the local Methodist church.

Unbelievably, by the time of the christening Mum was pregnant again. Everyone was horrified, but there was nothing to be done. The doctors were worried about Mum, who was exhausted a lot of the time, and ordered her to take as much rest as possible. This meant that a lot of the care of our baby sister was passed to us children, and as the oldest girl I was expected to do the lion's share.

We soon learned to feed Carole. Making up the bottles was not hard: there was no formula – she was simply given warm cow's milk; and there was no sterilising – we washed the bottles and teats under the tap. Later on we gave her watered down sweet tea in her bottles, and pieces of chopped apple to suck on and chew. We learned how to change the baby's nappies, soaking the dirty one in a bucket and then boiling them and hanging them on the small balcony outside the living room to dry. The worst part of looking after Carole was doing night feeds, because she was a restless baby who woke often. She was put in with Kim and me, so I would have to drag myself out of bed and stumble downstairs for a bottle as Carole bawled and the rest of the family slept on.

Christopher Ronald Ponting was born on 12 August 1964, just under a year after Carole. My first reaction was gratitude that he was not a girl and would not have to cater to Dad's appalling demands. But because he was a boy Dad had less interest in him and found him an irritation from the start. Thankfully he was born in hospital, where the medical staff insisted Mum be sterilised straight after the birth. This upset her a lot, but she agreed, reluctantly, after the doctors told her that her frail body simply could not sustain another pregnancy.

Sterilisation was a major operation in those days and Mum was kept in hospital for a couple of weeks after the birth, which meant a nightmare time for me. Dad brought the new baby home, handed him straight to me and had nothing more to do with him. At eight I was expected to look after both babies, as well as seeing to Dad's constant demands for tea, cigarettes, food and sexual gratification. Laurence and Kim did their best to help, but I could never bring myself to speak of Dad's persistent sexual abuse, especially to Laurence. I loved my brother so much that I could not bear to share my torture with him. Laurence looked on me as his pretty little sister, and we adored each other – and, indeed, he loved Kim too. The thought of him knowing that I was now damaged goods terrified me. I was afraid that if I told Laurence he would try to take revenge on Dad, and would only end up hurt. So I said nothing.

After seeing to the night feeds my day began at

6.30a.m. when I made bottles for Carole and Chris before cleaning the grate and lighting the fire in the living room. After that I made the tea and got the others up. Dad would bellow from the bedroom for his breakfast, and when I took it to him he would almost always force me into the bed with him.

Carole suffered constant eye infections which made her eyes seep with pus – we were forever wiping it away. She was just walking, though still in nappies, and we would hold her hand, one of us on each side, and take her with us when we went out to play. Chris was a lovely baby and everyone adored him. He turned out to be an easy and sweet-natured child, with dark hair and eyes, like Kim. I hauled him along in the pram with me wherever I went, proud because the neighbours would stop to coo over him.

Looking after the babies was the easy part of my day. Even making Dad's breakfast and supplying those endless cups of tea was not too bad. But in Mum's absence the abuse escalated and I spent my days in terror, dreading the next time Dad would bark out my name and order me to 'Fucking get in here and shut the door.' By this time he was abusing Kim regularly too, but it was still me he chose most often. We both knew what was going on, but we never talked about it – what could we say? It was as if we had an understanding between us, a silent empathy. We would let one another know, with a look, that we understood and were there for each other. Whether Laurence found out what Dad had been doing to us I shall never know. I cannot imagine Laurence knowing and not saying anything. But Dad was sly and clever. He was wary of Laurence, and would always make his attacks when our brother was out or late at night when everyone was asleep.

A few weeks after Mum came home from hospital she took Carole and Chris over to Auntie's. But if Mum was hoping that Auntie would take them in and provide for them in their infancy, as she had for the first three children, she was in for a shock. Auntie told Mum that she was too old to manage two more and simply could not do it. By this time Auntie was in her sixties, and although she told me later her heart ached when she saw the two little ones, she knew she had neither the energy nor the money to care for them. She told Mum she would continue to look after Laurence, Kim and me whenever possible, but not Carole or Chris.

No one could blame Auntie for her decision. It would have been beyond her to manage five children. I felt for Carole and Chris. Their lives were bleaker than ours; turned away by Auntie and by the Ponting grandparents, they had no one but Mum and Dad. There was no respite at all from the grim misery of life in Monteagle Court, and because this was all they knew, it was all they came to expect. Laurence, Kim and I knew there was something more. Auntie drummed it into us to 'hold your heads up high, be proud of yourselves and stand up for yourselves'. She taught us about cleanliness, godliness and kindness. She gave us a sense of direction, a belief that we were not all bad or useless, and hope for a better life in the future. Without that Carole and Chris were two little lost souls, their only examples to follow Mum, a browbeaten victim, and Dad, a vicious bully.

Apart from her infected eyes, Carole was absolutely plagued with nits. The problem was so bad that in the morning a black film of the little creatures would cover her pillow where her head had been. Kim and I tried to help by washing her pillow-case, and sometimes we managed to get hold of some nit shampoo to wash her hair – but even when we did, within a week or two the problem would be as bad as ever.

All of us had the usual childhood illnesses. If we were feeling really ill or we came out in spots Mum took us to Dr Perkins in a musty surgery in Pitfield Street, not far from the flats. The doctor was a stoutish man with greased-back black hair, a thin pencil moustache and glasses. He always wore a navy blue pinstriped suit with braces underneath, and sometimes a bow tie. Stern but kindly, very old-school and well educated, he was our doctor for many years, although we did not see him often and he never treated any of us for the injuries Dad inflicted – those were kept under wraps. If one of us got measles or mumps Dr Perkins would prescribe calamine lotion for the spots. Beyond that, we were expected to get on with it. From time to time, if one of us was really poorly, we would stay in bed and Mum would heat a tin of soup for us – but that was rare.

When Kim was six she had scarlet fever and Mum had to call Dr Perkins; it was the only time I ever remember him coming to the flat. Goodness knows what he made of the way we lived – he probably could not wait to get out again. Kim was ill for a long time and Laurence and I were sent to Auntie's for a while, where Auntie worried herself sick and pined for her little Black and Tan. Laurence was the most sickly of us all, with a weak chest as a result of the pneumonia he had had as a baby. He often coughed and wheezed, but no one took any notice. It was the same with the stammer he had developed very early on. It was probably a reaction to the fear and trauma he suffered at Dad's hands, but no one in our world bothered with things like that and he was just left to get on with it.

As for Carole, her bed-wetting was an even worse problem than her nits. She was potty trained by the age of two, but went on wetting the bed at night for years afterwards. The bedroom she shared with Kim and me stank of urine. We tried everything we could to stop her, putting a bowl by her bed every night and trying to wake her when we thought she needed to go. But nothing worked, and she developed nasty bedsores on her bottom and legs from lying in urine. When we could find the money, Kim and I would buy antiseptic cream to rub on them. In the mornings Mum would take the soaked sheets off the bed and hang them in front of the fire to dry without washing them, so that the living room stank of urine too. Sometimes Kim and I would try to wash the sheets in the bath, but it was impossible to do it every day and mostly we just had to live with the acrid smell, which seemed to permeate everything.

Even outside the flat our world seemed to be falling about our ears. One day bulldozers arrived to knock down the Secret F. We were heartbroken; our special playground was to disappear and there were very few other places we could go. The Jungle next door was to go too, along with the little parade of shops on the other side of the factory. It was all being cleared so that more flats could be built. Pat and Ted from the paper shop had been relocated, along with the doctor's surgery and a timber merchant, but Mrs Evans and her husband, the couple from the grocery, had decided to retire back to Wales. They had always been kind to us and we felt very sad.

We children stood watching as the bulldozers started work, fascinated by the size of them and the way they could knock down the old factory walls like a row of toy building bricks. Within a few hours there was nothing left but a patch of waste ground. I felt sorry for all the caterpillars in the Jungle – I hated the thought of them being crunched up by the bulldozer. The builders did not move in straightaway. Instead, a metal fence was erected round the site and a caretaker arrived to look after things. His name was George, and he spent his days in a small wooden shed. George was friendly to us children and, rather than shooing us off the site, let us play there and come into his shed for a chat while he brewed his tea over a tiny primus stove.

It was George who told us that the fair was coming to the site for a few days. All the local children were buzzing with the news: a real funfair, with all kinds of side-shows and the latest rides. We could not wait. This would be a whole different world from the forced 'fun' of Dad's outings. As soon as Dad heard about the fair, however, he banned us from going, insisting it was not safe. It was typical of him to stop us doing something we were looking forward to. He never allowed us to go on school trips, swimming, picnics or any outings he was not in charge of, and the arrival of the fair gave him another opportunity to deny us fun. We were bitterly disappointed. All the other kids were planning to be there on the first day of the fair, but we would be missing out once again. When they heard that we were not being allowed to go they laughed at us and said we were chicken, daring us to ignore our dad and go anyway.

It was just one more thing that set us apart. We were still targets for the other children just as we always had been, and we were sick of feeling different and being teased and taunted. There was a popular television programme at the time called *The Addams Family*, about a family of weirdos and monsters. It had a catchy little theme tune, and when Dad was beating Mum the kids would hear her shrieking and gather outside our front door, singing the words of the theme song and substituting 'the Ponting family' for 'the Addams family'. We hated it, and whenever I heard them I would run upstairs to our room with my fingers in my ears. Occasionally they went even further, ringing endlessly on our doorbell, putting black paint on the windows or sticking lighted matches through the letterbox. The shame and humiliation were awful, and being banned from the fair when everyone else was going seemed to seal our fate as outcasts. We could not bear it, so we decided we would fool Dad and sneak into the fair.

On the day the fair arrived we told Dad we were going out to play and headed towards the loud music and the bright lights. We wandered around, gazing wistfully at all the exciting rides and wishing we could have a go on some of them. Then George came to our rescue. He must have taken pity on us and he gave us half a crown – riches indeed. Kim and I knew exactly what we wanted to do with it and we headed for the brand-new parachute ride, a great big wheel reaching high into the air with little carriages on it that swung backwards and forwards as it spun round. Laurence agreed to look out for Dad while Kim and I climbed into one of the little carriages and, as the ride filled up, were hoisted higher and higher into the air.

We were right at the very top of the wheel, waiting for the ride to begin, when we saw Laurence signalling frantically. A moment later we saw Dad, prowling through the fairground looking for us. First he grabbed Laurence, and then he spotted Kim and me. Paralysed with fear, there was nothing we could do but wait for our turn to get off. I felt sick, knowing what was going to happen, and my stomach churned with dread. Dad stood below the ride, pointing his finger at us and then pointing to the ground, his face tight with fury. Those few minutes waiting to get off the ride were terrifying. The anticipation of what Dad would do was always awful, but this time it was even worse as we watched him waiting for us and knew there was no escape.

When we reached the ground Dad grabbed one of us in each hand, his fingers pinching the soft skin of our upper arms. People were watching, so he smiled as he pulled us along, pretending he was just taking us home for our tea. The beating we got was a bad one: we ached for days afterwards and the bruises took a long time to fade. But nothing was as awful as the gut-wrenching, skin-crawling, nauseating fear we had felt when we knew he was waiting for us.

But if Dad was organising a treat, of course, that was a different matter. My ninth birthday was approaching and I was not looking forward to it. Birthdays were never any fun in our house. We had no choice: Dad did the whole thing the way he wanted it. Mum would have been ordered to buy a fruit cake with 'Happy Birthday' in icing on the top from Andersen's, the bakers. He thought it impressed the neighbours. But I hated fruit cake and never ate any of it – it reminded me of Christmas pudding, which I loathed. To add insult to injury, everybody's birthday cake was bought with the money he always stole from inside their birthday cards from the few relatives who sent them to us. He would let Mum get us a small present, like some crayons or a ball, and the cake, and then he would pocket the rest of the cash for himself. We had to pretend to Nanny and Grandad Ponting and Aunt May and Uncle Wally that we had received the money, and visit them to say thank you.

Dad would usually suggest that we invite someone over for our 'party', but none of us could think of anyone to ask. Most of the children who lived round about did not like us, and we always refused to let anyone from school see the awful way we lived. But the year I turned nine I decided I would finally have a friend over, a girl called Vicky Gregory who lived in Flat 13. Vicky was one of the few kids who were nice to us. She came in a pretty party dress and brought me some clothes for a Cindy doll I had managed to hold on to from Christmas. From the moment she arrived I was painfully aware of how clean and nice Vicky looked and how shabby I was. The 'party' consisted of Kim, Laurence, Vicky and myself sitting at the table with a piece of the fruit cake each, with Mum hovering around and Dad eating the lion's share of the cake in front of the telly. Afterwards I took Vicky up to my room, but there was nothing there for us to do. She was very polite, though, and made no comment on the filth or the lack of toys. We sat on my bed and chatted until it was time for her to go.

A few days later Vicky asked me over to her house: I was really pleased and tried to make myself as clean as possible. Her home was a wonderland to me. The Gregorys were not rich, but Vicky's dad had always worked and compared to us they were loaded. Their flat was clean and nicely furnished, and Vicky's room was the most beautiful thing I had ever seen. The curtains and wallpaper matched her bedspread and pillow-cases, and she had a huge doll's house full of furniture and a pink portable record-player. There was a lovely soft carpet on the floor and all kinds of books, crayons and other toys. As I took in the luxury all I could think was that I should never have asked her to our flat. I shrank with embarrassment and shame, knowing that she had seen the squalor and grime we lived in. Vicky's mum was very kind and served us squash and sandwiches as we sat in the pink bedroom, threading coloured beads on to strings and listening to her brother's Beatles records. It was one of the best afternoons I had ever had. I felt I was in a magic spell until the moment I had to go back and the reality of my own home set in once more.

I wished I could go over to Vicky's all the time, but I was far too ashamed to ask her to our flat again and so the friendship did not really have a chance. We played together outside sometimes, and I used to look up at her window, imagining the beautiful room inside and dreaming that it was mine. Indeed, one of my greatest strengths was my imagination, for being able to dream helped me survive. I would dream of being grown up and free, and that gave me something to look forward to. I knew that, if I could get through to the day I left home, I would find a way to make a good life for myself. I would get a job and a nice home and have clean, new clothes and all the things I longed for.

I spent hours day-dreaming. My favourite was the unexpected knock on the door. The woman on the doorstep would be beautiful and kind and would tell me I had been adopted and that she was my real mum who had been in another country and had now come for me. Sometimes I would vary the dream by imagining I had been accidentally swapped at birth and my real mum had finally tracked me down. Occasionally I dreamed of being an angel. Someone had once told me a story about God's little angels, and how children who died young went to a beautiful garden and had gossamer wings they could float about on. From the day I heard that story I wanted to be an angel so much that I could almost smell the flowers.

Kim dreamed, too. One time when Dad took us on an outing to Southend we looked up at the cliff face and saw hundreds of little coloured lights scattered through the trees and bushes. 'Those are fairies at work,' I told Kim. 'They're busy getting things ready for Santa Claus.' Kim's little face shone. 'Do they only come at Christmas, or can fairies give you wishes?' she asked. I told her they could. For a while she was deep in thought.

'What did you ask for?' I asked her. 'I can't tell you,' she said. 'If I do, it won't come true.'

It wasn't hard to guess what Kim had wished for. The same things as me: love, food and for our bad dad to go away.

8

Growing Up

George, the factory-site caretaker who had enabled us to go to the fair, was a friend to all the children and we would often go and visit him in his little hut. The waste ground was a great short cut through to the market and we all used it. One day I decided to go over and visit him, climbing through the hole in the fence as usual. I had some-how managed to escape Dad's clutches and did not dare go home for the next few hours. As it was a drizzly, cold day, George's hut would offer a bit of welcome shelter until I thought it was safe to return.

Busy brewing up, George, welcomed me with his usual friendly smile and chat. He sat me on the small stool near the paraffin heater in the corner of the hut and handed me a mug of tea. At that moment I felt something change, and I suddenly felt tense and anxious. George had come a little too close and was asking me whether I had a boyfriend. The look on his face reminded me of Dad – and then he tried to put an arm round me. The next moment he grabbed my face in his hands and tried to kiss me, full on.

I felt sick and shocked. Not George! Surely nice, kind old George wasn't doing this? Were all men like this, or was it just me who made them want to hurt me? I grabbed the door handle, pulled it open and ran out, tears streaming down my cheeks. Now I could never go to George's hut again. I had thought he was a friend, but I was wrong. I wandered around in the rain for hours before going home soaked, bedraggled and cold. That night I took the kitchen scissors and hacked off as much as I could of my long blonde hair. If I was ugly, maybe men like George and Dad would leave me alone.

Where Dad was concerned, Kim and I now began to realise that we could sometimes find ways to foil him when he wanted to play 'games' with us. Feisty and determined to stop him, we spent a lot of time working out strategies. When I had to take his tea up to him in the morning Kim would go to the front door and knock hard and then scream that the postman was at the door. That always worked – Dad would be hoping for a giro or benefit money of some kind, so I would offer to see what it was and rush downstairs again. I would open and shut the door and then call out to him that it was a mistake, or just some junk mail. Then I would rush to get ready for school before he could call me upstairs again.

Another of the ways we found of escaping him was by climbing out of our parents' bedroom window on to the flat roof outside. When Dad called us into the living room during the day or evening, which he often did when Mum was out, we would run into their room, open the window and climb out. From the roof we could climb across to the staircase which led down to the ground floor and then leg it for the next few hours, until we knew Mum was back and the danger past.

When Mum was out, Dad would often call Kim and me into the living room so that he could choose which one of us he was going to have his way with. He would toy with us, making us wait, knowing that we were both terrified. 'Mum's out for a while,' he would say, 'so what shall we do? Shall we get the big coat and cuddle under it?' Usually Dad chose me to stay and let Kim go. But neither of us wanted to leave the other to his clutches, so the one who was not that day's victim would hang around, playing for time and hoping Mum would get back. Sometimes if I had to stay with Dad Kim would bang on the front door or shout, 'Mum's coming' to get him to stop.

But although we grew clever at avoiding him we could not always manage to do so, and he was still forcing us to do things which hurt us and turned our stomachs. Getting us to give him oral sex was his favourite. When I was with him he would hold me by the hair and force my face into his groin. I choked and gagged, but I was a small child and he had the strength of a grown man, so there was nothing I could do.

One day Mum went to see a friend who was sick. Dad called Kim and me into the living room, but we immediately put a plan in place. I told Kim that, if she would try and distract Dad, I would get out, find Mum and bring her home. So I told Dad I needed to go to the toilet and left the room. I pulled the chain and then tried to slip quickly out of the front door while the flushing noise was still going on. But I had not counted on our door latch, which always stuck, and I was still struggling with it when the flush stopped. Kim heard me and started to cough loudly to give me cover. I knew Dad would realise after a few minutes that I had gone and I was worried sick about Kim, left alone with him. But she was good at making excuses and putting Dad off, so I knew that with any luck she would hold him at bay while I found Mum and got her to come home. Although I am sure Mum had a good idea what Dad did to us, he always stopped when she came home.

It was a good five miles to Mare Street, where Mum's friend Vera lived. I had no money for a bus and ran most of the way. When I got there Mum was surprised to see me and asked what on earth I was doing. She, too, had managed to escape from home, by saying she was going to borrow money from Vera, and now she was enjoying a cup of tea and a gossip. Vera had cancer and her yellow skin and popped-out features scared me, so I tried not to look at her. I told Mum that Dad wanted her home straightaway, knowing it would make her come with me. Mum was really fed up about this, but she came, and as she had got some money from Vera we got the bus back. Waiting at the bus-stop, Mum chatted on about Vera while I tried to think of a way to tell her what I needed to say.

I had decided that I simply had to talk to Mum about what Dad was doing, because if I told her she just might be able to do something. I don't know what, because Mum was powerless in our house and totally under Dad's control. But I was desperate to find a way to stop Dad doing the disgusting things he did to Kim and me and Mum seemed to be my only hope. I had still said nothing when we got to our stop. We headed over to the blue shop, where Mum bought some cigarettes from Dolly, and when we came out of the shop I knew it was now or never. I blurted out that Dad wanted Kim and me to play nasty games and that he hurt us and now Kim was on her own with him and we needed to hurry.

Mum grabbed my hand and almost frog-marched me down Hare Walk. When we reached the flat, Kim and I were sent upstairs. Kim told me that she had kept Dad off her by telling him that I had gone to get Mum. Downstairs, a huge row erupted between Mum and Dad. We held our breath. Would anything change?

We were crazy even to hope. In my heart of hearts, I knew she would stick by Dad. She would have had to be mad or incredibly stupid not to have known what was going on long before I told her. She just did not want to know. With life the way it was with Dad, it was easier for her to choose him over us. I felt bitterly let down. This time, more than any other, I had needed Mum to come through for us. When she failed to do so, I felt I had lost any love I had for her. Although I still pitied her, a part of me began to despise her for putting up with Dad and letting him hurt us so badly. Most of all, I knew I would never ask her for her help again. I was on my own.

And so, if no one was going to believe us or help us, we decided that at least we would find ways to take our revenge on Dad. Kim and I were both little rebels with a wicked streak and a powerful will to survive and, although we were still terrified of him, getting back at him, even in small ways, made us feel a lot better.

Once Dad asked us to make him a bacon sandwich, so we cooked the bacon and then rubbed it on the filthy kitchen floor, giggling like mad as we did, before putting it between two slices of bread for him. Another time he wanted a salmon salad. Dad's idea of a salad was lettuce, cucumber, tomato, radishes and beetroot arranged on a plate, with the tinned salmon in the middle. He always insisted it was a special treat, because things like cucumber were expensive then, but we hated it. He never let us have condiments of any kind – sauces, ketchup and dressings were banned because he did not like them, and the salad tasted awful without anything on it. He would force us to eat every last bite, so we took enormous delight in adding some snot to the salmon on his plate before serving it up to him.

We thought of all kinds of tricks like this, putting the most disgusting things we could think of in his food and then trying not to giggle as we watched him eat it. We would rub his bacon on our dirty feet or stamp on it, spit in his tea and, when Buster the dog was with us, rub his bread on Buster's belly. The funny thing was that he hardly ever noticed. Once in a while he would say, 'This tastes a bit funny', and we would reply, 'Oh, it's a different kind of bacon' or whatever other excuse we could think of. Usually he would finish it up, while we went outside and laughed till our sides hurt.

One Christmas, Kim and I had to cook the lunch. We got the huge turkey out of the oven and accidentally dropped it on the floor. Dad heard the crash and shouted, 'What was that?' but we yelled, 'Nothing! Don't worry – just a pan', and quickly scooped the bird off the floor. We stuck it in the sink and washed the grit, hairs and grime off it and then put it back in the pan and served it up. We both asked for just a small piece of the inside flesh and then watched Dad tuck into the skin, catching one another's eye and grinning at the thought of where it had been.

As we got older we decided that, great as it was watching him eat snot or dirt off the floor, it was not enough. We began to hatch all kinds of plans to kill him. We discussed stabbing him with scissors or getting hold of his airgun and shooting him in the temple. Finally we came up with what we thought was a brilliant plan – we would poison him. With a bit of money earned by taking a neighbour's washing to the laundrette we bought the most poisonous things we could think of – some Bob Martin's dog distemper tablets from the local petshop.

The tablets had a thick yellow coating, which we painstakingly scraped off over several days, before grinding them into a powder. That night Dad asked for a coffee and we tipped the ground tablets into it. We watched with bated breath while Dad sipped the coffee and then made a face. 'This tastes odd,' he snapped. 'What have you put in it?' 'Nothing, Dad,' we chorused. 'It's just the usual coffee.' He made a few more faces, but to our amazement and delight he drank the lot.

That night we waited, hoping desperately that we would find him dead in the morning. Instead we heard him head for the toilet, groaning and complaining about his guts. Dad spent most of the next day on the toilet, but, apart from gut-ache and an upset stomach, much to our disappointment our attempts to bump him off came to nothing.

Kim and I still never talked to one another about what was happening. We talked about ways to avoid Dad, but not about what he was doing. We had no need to – we both knew, and we would offer each other support in silent ways. It might be a sympathetic look, or an extra potato passed over at dinner, or a pat on the back – enough to let the other know we were on her side. Those little gestures of comfort said it all.

Humour was what helped us most. We would laugh together about the tricks we played on Dad and how horrible he was. Somehow we both knew we would survive and that it would not always be like this. On summer evenings we would sit in the open window of our room to escape the perpetual smell of urine and filth, and look at the stars and dream. We would talk about what we were going to do, the husbands we would meet, the jobs we would get, the travels we would go on, and what life would be like when we escaped the horrors of Monteagle Court.

Laurence, who was already able to escape into

his own world and did not have to suffer sexual abuse as we girls did, found further solace in a newcomer to our household. One of the 'uncles' who visited Mum, when Dad needed her to earn some money, was a man called Alf. Taller and bigger than Dad, and not in the least afraid of him, Alf was no looker. He had a huge, hooked nose and a set of uneven teeth, his clothes never seemed to fit his gangly body properly, and he wore the most enormous, ugly boots on his huge feet. But under his rough exterior Alf had a heart of gold. He was friendly, kind and polite and we kids loved his visits because he was always nice to us and would stop for a chat and slip us some sweets before disappearing upstairs with Mum.

Although Dad encouraged Mum to have sex with other men for money, he disliked Alf. Dad had to behave himself when he was around because Alf would have picked him up in one huge hand and tossed him across the room if he had caught Dad beating us. But Dad put up with Alf because he wanted the money. One evening Alf turned up at the door and told Mum and Dad he had been evicted from his lodgings. He asked whether he could stay for a while and offered to pay rent. Since there was money involved Dad agreed, and Alf and his sleeping bag moved into Laurence's room.

Having Alf in the house made a big difference. He did not seem to mind the state of the place, perhaps because he was at work all day or perhaps because being near Mum mattered more to him. Clean, tidy and very generous, he never looked at us children in a strange way or tried to touch us. He was genuinely interested in what we were doing and would often bring us little treats.

Alf soon formed a special friendship with Laurence. He would take him fishing, play chess with him and chat to him for hours about music and cars. Alf played the guitar, which Laurence loved, and Alf was delighted when our brother showed a natural aptitude for music. The two of them became pals, and Laurence found in Alf the father-figure he had never had. I was jealous of their friendship and wished I had someone to take a special interest in me. Alf was always kind to us girls, bringing us sweets or crisps after a day out fishing, but it was Laurence he liked best.

Looking back, it is easy to see that Alf was in love with Mum. There was no doubt that they were carrying on a relationship while Alf was living with us, which Dad tolerated because it brought him money. Mum was dowdy and shapeless after five kids and living such a squalid existence with Dad for so long, but Alf would pay attention to her, telling her she looked nice and treating her to little presents. Many times I saw him looking at her with real fondness in his eyes. I am sure Alf would have liked Mum to leave and set up home with him, but she was never going to leave Dad. By this time she was too downtrodden, too deeply under his control to break away, even for the offer of a far better, kinder man. Alf moved out after a while, but returned regularly and stayed for days or even weeks so that he could be around Mum.

But even outside our family, people like Alf were a rarity in our lives. At best we were ignored; more often, bullied or taken advantage of. Because we had so few possessions – a toy was a rarity, and anything pretty or special for ourselves was out of the question – we often stood outside shops, looking at the things inside and imagining what it would be like to own them. One of the things I longed for was a signet ring, which to me seemed the most special thing you could have. Many children we knew were allowed them, but for us there was no chance.

The ring I wanted was in a jeweller's near Auntie's. It cost three pounds – a huge sum, but I decided to save up and get it. I already did a paper round, and asked at the shop if I could do extra rounds. Although we had to hand most of our earnings over to Dad, I was able to save some of the extra money in a little purse I kept under my mattress. Whenever I was at Auntie's I went to the jeweller's to gaze at the ring in the window. One day I even plucked up the courage to go in and try it on. The shop assistant was kind when I told her I was saving up for it, and told me to come back when I had enough.

It took months of effort, but in the end all my threepenny bits and sixpences added up to the sum I needed. I went to the shop. I peered into the window. The ring was gone. I went in and the kindly assistant told me it had been sold. I was devastated. Tears filled my eyes. Nothing ever came easy, and even hard work and extra chores resulted in disappointment. But the shop assistant patted my arm. 'Don't worry, we'll get another in soon. Pop back next week,' she said. I did, and to my surprise and joy there was an identical ring.

I paid the money and took the bag that held the ring in a little black box. Over the moon, I skipped all the way to Auntie's. At last I had something I truly wanted. When I arrived at Auntie's and produced the box, I opened it to show her – but there was no ring. What had happened? I had not dropped it. I had not opened it. The only explanation was that the shop assistant must have dropped it in the shop.

I ran all the way back. Breathless and agitated, I went in and asked her about my ring. The girl just stared at me and denied that it had fallen out in the shop. She assured me she had placed it in the box. But she avoided my eyes and I knew she was lying. She called the manager, who insisted that what I was saying was impossible. As so often in my young life, one adult believed another and I was simply perceived as a hysterical child.

I sobbed, but it made no impact on the uncaring pair. The manager led me to the door, opened it and ushered me out. As I left I turned around and the sales assistant looked at me with a triumphant smile on her face. I knew I was right, but I could do nothing. It seemed that every time I dared to hope or to look forward to something I was let down. I felt I could trust no one – life was cruel and unfair, and no one cared. Once again, I was on my own.

But kids learn, and kids grow up. My turn would come. In the meantime, it was my brother who was presented with an opportunity of distancing himself a bit more from our dreadful environment. Laurence had turned eleven and it was decided that he would sit the eleven plus exam, which, if he passed, would enable him to go to a good secondary school. He was a bright boy with a special aptitude for maths, and his teachers had encouraged him to work hard. They knew how difficult his home circumstances were, but they also knew that he had Auntie's backing and when she came to the school they told her how good his prospects were. Despite his stammer and his shyness, Laurence had a lot of charm. Although he never got on especially well with the other kids, adults loved him because he was quiet and polite. A self-contained, academic boy, he would often be reading or listening to the news, he found figures fascinating and he was always learning.

I adored Laurence and had always looked up to him – to me he was invincible. I always felt safer when he was around because he looked out for Kim and me and did his best to protect us. After Chris arrived, Laurence spent a lot of time with him. The two of them shared a small bedroom which Laurence worked hard to keep clean and tidy. He would spend some of the money he earned from paper rounds and deliveries on model aeroplanes which he and Chris spent hours putting together, locked away in their room. It was easy to see that Laurence was headed in a different direction to most of the children from our background, and when he passed his eleven plus with flying colours it was proposed that he try for entry to the London Nautical School in Blackfriars. The school was geared to training boys for the Navy, and since Laurence had long since decided that he wanted to be a fighter pilot in the Navy, getting into the school would be his dream come true.

While Mum and Dad showed barely any interest, Auntie was determined to give Laurence his chance. When the letter arrived giving him an interview date, she took him out and bought him some smart new clothes. Her determination to help Laurence was such that she went back on her word and visited Monteagle Court to make sure our parents would make the effort. I was scared for her, thinking Dad would throw her out, but he had decided that the forthcoming interview was a chance for him to create an impression as a proud father. He ordered himself a new suit from one of his catalogues, and even took one of his rare baths. When Laurence heard in due course that he had got into the school he was thrilled. Even better, Dad agreed to let him live with Auntie during the week, so that he would only have to return home at weekends.

Laurence was on his way. He had a bright future in a good school and was living with Auntie. I was happy for him, and proud of him too, but knowing he would be gone for most of the time left me feeling very lonely – I was going to miss him terribly. And without Laurence around, even more of the burden of coping with Dad's violence and caring for the little ones would fall on me. I wondered if I would ever be as lucky as Laurence. I knew I was clever – though not as academic as he was – and I longed for a similar opportunity to go to a good school and escape from home. But would it come?

9

Crises

At ten I was approaching adolescence and Dad was loving it. He was obsessed with how many pubic hairs I had, and my newly growing breasts. I was desperate to get away from him, but his horrible demands went on and, although I was growing bigger, I was still no match for him. He was heavily into pornography and probably always had been, but I had been too young to notice, let alone understand, before. Now that we were old enough to be embarrassed by it, Dad enjoyed making Kim and me play cards with him using pornographic playing cards. He also made us watch a porn film called *The French Maid*, which we found quite funny because the projector speeded the film up so that the 'maid', who flounced about in her little apron and nothing else, bobbed about at a ludicrous speed.

Dad had few friends, but he had one called Ronnie who was a real spiv. He was good-looking, in an arrogant way, with his jet-black oiled quiff, piercing blue eyes and smart clothes. He reeked of cheap aftershave and swaggered about, convinced that he was irresistible to women. Dad and Ronnie obviously had a lot in common. Together they bought photographic processing equipment and set it up in the bathroom, where they would spend hours developing photos they took with their smart new camera. Sometimes Ronnie's wife, Paula, came round too. She looked like a pretty young woman who had aged too fast; life with Ronnie and three kids had obviously taken its toll on her. When Ronnie and Paula came round we were often shooed out of the house for several hours, and when we came back Dad and Ronnie would be upstairs locked in the bathroom with their photo equipment.

We had no idea what they were doing until one day Kim and I, rooting through a kitchen drawer for something, came across a pile of photos. At first we could not work out what they were – there seemed to be all kinds of body parts on show, and bodies all tangled up together. Eventually the light dawned – it was Mum, Dad, Ronnie and Paula, all stark naked in every possible pornographic pose in various combinations with one another. We were very shocked, especially by the sight of Mum in these graphic sexual poses. We knew Dad had to be behind it, but why on earth had Mum agreed? We were not sure what to do, and in the end we just stuffed the photos back in the drawer. We both pretended to find it funny, but I think deep inside we were very upset and wished we had never discovered their horrible secret.

A few weeks later Ronnie and Paula turned up on our doorstep with their three children: they had been evicted and needed a place to stay. Alf was back with us and there was really no room, but Dad agreed to take them in. Alf and Chris continued to share Laurence's old room, while Ronnie, Paula and their baby slept in the living room and their ten-year-old daughter and son came in with Kim, Carole and me. The flat was jam-packed, and it was hard for us because we did not like Ronnie and Paula's kids any more than we liked the parents. The daughter was rude and sullen; she hated staying with us and made no attempt to hide the fact. The only good thing was that while they were all with us Dad could not get Kim or me alone, so we were safe. For that it would have been worth sharing our room with ten horrible daughters.

A few weeks later Ronnie and Paula were offered a new three-bedroom maisonette on the lower two floors of a house in Dalston where they would also have a large back garden. Their daughter was cock-a-hoop about leaving the 'shit-hole', as she called our flat, and having a room of her own. I was delighted to see the back of the whole family. Ronnie had begun to sit a little too close to me on the sofa and to give me the kind of looks which set off warning bells in my head – his handsome face had taken on a sinister air. Left minding all the younger children for the whole day while Mum and Dad helped Ronnie and Paula move, I comforted myself with the thought that we would never have to see them again.

But, much to my surprise, Mum and Dad, who never went anywhere, began visiting Ronnie and Paula in their new home. I had no idea why, but I suspected that money must be involved somewhere along the line. Money was Dad's one and only motivation. If there was money to be made he would do anything – including, as I was soon to discover, selling his own kids.

A couple of months after Ronnie and Paula moved out Dad told me I was coming with him and Mum to visit them. He told me to have a wash and put on my best clothes and, with a hideous wink, said there was going to be a surprise for me. My heart sank. I hated the thought of seeing them again and I could not imagine that the surprise would be anything nice; but I knew I had no choice, so I put on a cotton frock Auntie had given me and we set off.

We got off the bus close to Dalston Junction station and, after a ten-minute walk, arrived in a pretty tree-lined road with houses on either side. As we reached Ronnie and Paula's house I noticed a curtain twitch in the house opposite, and for a second I caught a glimpse of a man's face watching us. We walked down a path at the side of the house to the front door where Ronnie was waiting for us, all smiles and jokes. 'You go up and see my girl,' he told me, while Mum and Dad followed him into the living room.

I hated her, but I had to do as I was told, so I went slowly up the stairs. When I got to the top I caught sight of her in one of the bedrooms. She was sitting at a big old dressing table, putting on make-up. And she was naked. 'Come on,' she told me. 'Get undressed. They're waiting for us.' She was a pretty little girl, but she looked grotesque and comical in the blue eye-shadow and red lipstick which she had applied in crooked, childish smudges.

I failed to understand and looked at her blankly. With the exasperated air of a seasoned hand explaining procedures to a new apprentice, she filled me in. 'They're making a film and you and me are the stars. Your dad's gonna fuck me, and my dad's gonna fuck you. I don't know why – normally it's just me and my dad. But we'll get more money if there's two of us. So get a move on.' With that she got up and, without a hint of embarrassment, said, 'See you downstairs' and headed out of the room.

A moment later I heard Dad's voice, screaming at me to get undressed and put on some lipstick. Horrified, and very frightened, I ran downstairs. I could hear voices in the front room, but the door was closed and I headed for the front door. However, before I could open it Ronnie emerged from the living room, naked and with a huge erection. He must have seen the horror on my face, and, realising that I was not intending to play ball, grabbed me by the hair, whacked me and then started to force my clothes off, muttering, 'Love a fighter' as he held me by my neck against the kitchen wall. 'Your dad tells me you ain't broken in yet – we're gonna have a lot of fun,' he said, grinning. Meanwhile I fought as hard as I could, kicking and biting to stop him getting my clothes off. Despite my efforts I would not have stood a chance against him, but, mercifully, at that moment there was a knock at the door and a voice said, 'Police! Open up.'

Ronnie panicked and shoved me into the front room where I was greeted by the horrific sight of his daughter, bent over the arm of the pink sofa with my naked father behind her, a leer on his face, panting and gasping as he raped her. Ronnie's young daughter, a child who had been so abused and corrupted that she had no comprehension of the atrocity that was being committed on her, was smiling. And both mothers, hers and mine, were across the room, cheering them on and filming the whole scene. Numb with horror and panic, I knew I was never going to let them do that to me, ever.

Bedlam broke out as Ronnie hastily got his clothes on and went to open the door, while the little girl was rushed upstairs and the camera equipment hidden. I heard Ronnie, all charm and laughter, talking to the police at the door. I pushed out of the room and said to the policeman, 'Excuse me, sir.' He turned to me and said, 'Who asked you to open your mouth?' and then turned back to Ronnie. A few minutes later the door closed and he came back into the room. The police had bought his story that nothing was going on, and had not even bothered to come inside and check. But it had given Ronnie, Paula, Mum and Dad enough of a fright that they decided to end filming for the day, and we left. As we went out Ronnie grinned at me and said, 'Another time, soon, eh?'

Dad was furious: he would have made good money out of me. Despite all his sordid interference he had never had intercourse with me, and this meant I was worth a lot of money. I heard him talking to Mum about it, cursing the police and whoever had called them. As we walked away I looked up and saw the curtain opposite twitching again, and behind it the smiling face of my guardian angel, an old man who was giving me a thumbs-up sign.

On the way home I did not speak, and when we got back I went up to my room and lay on the bed. I still felt numb. There were no depths to which Dad would not stoop. And Mum had been part of it too. I knew he had talked her into it, with the promise of all the money they would make. There had been times when she had tried to help us in the past, but now I realised she was as bad as he was – both of them would sink to such depths that they would sell their own kids for sex. This was what they were up to with Ronnie and Paula, making porn films that they could sell and presumably splitting the proceeds. I hated them all. I thought about running away – but where would I go? And I could not leave Kim and the little ones.

For reasons I shall never know, but for which I am eternally grateful, Mum and Dad never tried to involve me in their sordid films again. Perhaps they could not be bothered with a little rebel like me when there were compliant children they could use. Perhaps they were afraid I would tell the authorities. Whatever the reason, I had made a vow to myself that I would die rather than let them do the things that were done to Ronnie's daughter. Despite everything, Dad had never had full sex with me – yet he was prepared to do it with another young child. Had he been saving me for something like this? I wondered.

Though they never mentioned it to me again they continued to visit Ronnie and Paula, and to have them over to our flat. I used to loathe Ronnie's leers and winks every time he came in. Then we children would be sent out of the way while they got on with their sickening games and film-making.

One day, when Ronnie and Paula were coming over, Dad gave me the money to go to the cinema. Kim was at a friend's house and a neighbour was watching Carole and Chris, so I was on my own. I was excited about going to see a film and walked down to the local picture house where they were showing a new musical. Dad, keen to buy my silence about what they were up to, had given me enough for a Kia-ora orange drink and some popcorn and the cinema was almost empty, so I took my goodies and found a seat in the middle of a row.

Just before the film started a man came in and sat next to me. I felt agitated. There were loads of empty seats, so why would he sit right beside me like that? I thought about moving, but did not want to seem rude. A few minutes into the film the man slipped his hand on to my knee and started to move it up under my dress. I froze in horror. What should I do? I looked around, but the few other people in the cinema were engrossed in the film. I pushed his hand away and ran out, leaving my popcorn and drink behind.

Outside the cinema I burst into tears. Why did these horrible things keep happening to me? For the rest of the day I wandered the streets, trying to while away the time until I was allowed home again at 6p.m. When at last I felt it was safe to go home I reached our road and saw Alf coming towards me, suitcase in hand. He had been staying with us for the last few days.

'I can't stay no more, Jenny,' he told me. 'I asked your mum to come with me, but she won't. And after what I've seen them get up to today, I can't stay. Tell Laurence I'll keep in touch.' He kissed my cheek and went on up the street, shoulders bowed.

When I got home I could not look at Mum and Dad. He was sitting in front of the TV as though nothing had happened, and she was making tea. I told them I had seen Alf. 'He didn't like our games,' Dad said, grinning and dragging on his cigarette. I went up to my room, despising the pair of them for the sickening things I knew they had been doing and for driving away a good man like Alf, my brother's surrogate father-figure.

Laurence had started at the Naval College and looked wonderfully grown up and handsome in his smart uniform and white cap. We hardly ever saw him any more unless Kim and I were sent to Auntie's, when it would be the three of us and her again just as always. Although he appeared for the odd weekend, he stayed with Auntie as much as he could. Dad insisted he came home for Christmas and New Year, however, and when he did things came to a head between them.

Perhaps it was the contrast between Alf and Dad,

or Laurence's growing confidence now that he was at the Naval College. Or perhaps it was simply that Laurence was growing up, and the skinny little boy who had been bullied and humiliated by Dad for so many years was becoming bigger and stronger. Whatever it was, the day came when Laurence's hatred of Dad came to the boil and he was prepared to take no more.

It was New Year's Eve and Dad was laying into Mum, snarling and swearing at her while raining punches on her head and body. She was screaming for us to help her and Kim and I were trying to pull Dad off her and at the same time avoid being hit ourselves. Suddenly Laurence came into the room, his face red with fury. He yelled at us to move away, and there was something in his tone of voice that made us obey instantly. Head down to avoid the blows, he launched himself at Dad, shouting, 'Leave her alone, you bastard.' Over and over again he threw himself on Dad, kicking and punching him with all the strength he could find. Dad was taken by surprise and backed away, swearing at Laurence and clutching his bruised legs. Laurence had a look of triumph on his face that I had never seen before. His wrist was fractured and his nose broken, but at that moment he did not care. He had stood up to his monster of a father and things would never be the same between them again.

Dad retreated, snarling, to his chair and his

cigarettes, telling us all to fuck off. Kim and I got Laurence to the hospital where he was patched up and then took him to Auntie's, where we knew she would nurse him. Despite his pain Laurence was not sorry – he only wished he had hurt Dad more. Clearly shaken by what had happened, after that incident Dad was only too glad for Laurence to stay at Auntie's as much as possible. As for me, I worshipped my brother even more than I had before.

Soon we realised that the medical staff at the hospital had reported to the authorities that Laurence had received injuries caused by his father. Refusing to pretend it was an accident, Laurence had told them the truth, and a couple of days later an NSPCC officer turned up at our door. Kim and I were excited. At last, someone whose job it was to protect kids. Surely he would help us, ask us the truth, listen to us. We could not wait.

Mum took him in to the living room with Dad and we waited while they talked for half an hour. Then the door opened and the man came out, said a cheery goodbye to Mum and Dad and left. We could not believe it. He had not even asked to meet us, let alone listened to anything we had to say. He was just like all the others – the police and the social workers. They only listened to Mum and Dad, and we kids were ignored.

Of course Dad would have spun him a line about

how hard it was bringing up all these children, and how Laurence's injuries had been caused accidentally when he was trying to restrain his unruly son. Perhaps the NSPCC inspector was not totally taken in because he continued to visit us regularly, to keep an eye on things. But he always spent his time with Mum and Dad; we were never allowed to be present.

I lay in bed at night wondering whether to approach him and whether he would believe me if I did. In the end I knew I had to try one more time to get help. I spent hours working out how I could do so without Dad knowing. The NSPCC man came pretty often – I am sure Mum and Dad must have had hand-outs from the charity, otherwise he would not have been tolerated. But I never knew when his next visit would be, so for days after I hatched my plan my stomach was rumbling with fear and my mind was in turmoil as I waited for him to appear.

When he finally did show up I waited at the top of the stairs while he talked to Mum and Dad. Eventually I heard the living room door open and ran quickly down, offering to see him out. Dad agreed and I walked with him to the door, where I said as quietly as I could, 'Can I talk to you?' Missing the signs completely, he took my hand and led me straight back into the living room where he said cheerfully, 'Jenny has got something she'd like to talk about.' I panicked, knowing I had to think fast, and made up a story about someone who was bullying me at school. He told me to hold my chin up and asked Mum and Dad to keep a close eye on things. Then he left.

Devastated, I watched him go, knowing that yet another adult had let me down. Later I tortured myself by thinking that I had handled things all wrong. Maybe he would have listened if I had said I wanted to speak to him alone, or had managed to follow him outside and talk there. But then again, maybe not. His attitude seemed to be that whatever I had to say could be said in front of my parents.

After this failed attempt to talk to someone in authority I felt trying to get help was hopeless. If even a child protection officer did not listen to children, what else was there? Was no one ever going to pay me any attention? Would things never get any better? I had done my best and it had not worked. I felt very, very alone.

But maybe, as with Laurence, education would offer a ray of hope. I was now in my last year at primary school and in Miss Tinline's class. Miss Tinline had been his teacher the year before and had helped him to do so well. I was good at sports and got into the swimming, netball and rounders teams. Several times I won trophies for the school, especially for swimming – all those trips to Highbury pool when we were at Auntie's had paid off and I was a strong swimmer, which won me respect from the boys as well as the girls. I also got lots of certificates for being a monitor and helping in the classroom, which made me feel very proud.

Mum and Dad had no interest in how I was doing at school, and I was glad. The last thing I wanted was them turning up at school and shaming me in front of the teachers and the other kids. When we were given letters to take home, inviting our parents to plays or open evenings, I threw them away just in case Dad decided to take a sudden interest and turn up to 'impress' the teachers. Both Kim and I used to pretend that other parents were ours. We would pick out some smartly dressed, nice-looking woman in the audience at the school concert and then nudge our friends and tell them that she was our Mum.

On one occasion Auntie came to an open evening for Kim and me. She dressed us both in beautiful velvet dresses and held our hands as we walked into the school. We both made sure all our friends saw us and knew we were with Auntie, who looked so smart and proud beside us. She listened intently to what all the teachers said about each of us, and gave our hands a little squeeze when they praised us. She was so proud of us and we were so chuffed that she came; we felt really special. But that was the only time Auntie was able to come, because Dad found out and banned her from appearing at the school again. Yet she still cheered us on for every achievement, and having her backing and support made a world of difference.

I took my eleven plus and did well in the English and history sections, but failed the maths. I was very disappointed; Auntie had wanted me to go to the Lady Owen School for Girls in Islington. I wanted to go there too, mainly because it was closer to Auntie's flat and would mean I could spend most of my time with her as Laurence did. Instead I was sent for an interview at Haggerston Secondary Modern, an all-girl school with a reasonable reputation which was close to Monteagle Court. I did well in my interview and was one of four girls from Burbage Primary to be offered a place there. I looked forward to it, for I was longing to grow up and leave home.

In the meantime there were still horrors to be faced on the home front, sometimes occurring at the most unexpected moments. In the spring after I turned eleven I heard the most exciting news – I was going to be a bridesmaid that summer for Uncle Dave, Dad's brother. Nanny and Grandad, grateful to be getting their youngest son off their hands at last, were pushing the boat out and organising a grand wedding. I was to be one of six bridesmaids and Laurence was to be a page-boy. Wild with excitement, my imagination ran riot. It was to be my first ever wedding and a dream come true. I spent hours picturing myself in my beautiful dress, floating along behind the bride.

In reality I did not like Mary, the bride, at all. She was an unattractive girl with buck teeth who was horrid to me. Dave was not much better – he was a carbon copy of Dad, even down to the speech impediment and spittle-covered mouth, and I found him creepy. I decided they deserved each other. But my dislike of the bride and groom did not spoil my dreams in the least – it would still be a glorious occasion and I would look just like a princess in a fairy tale.

This was the biggest event in the Ponting social calendar for ages. Laurence and I were taken for endless fittings. My dress was a gorgeous sky blue with lots of lacy underskirts, and I was also going to wear a coronet of blue and white flowers in my hair and little white ballet shoes. So full of excitement was I that I talked about being a bridesmaid non-stop, without realising how hard it must have been for Kim. She had been left out, and no one gave her a second thought. With her dark looks she failed to fit the Ponting ideal of the blonde, blue-eyed child, and she was often treated as second-best by Dad and the rest of his family. Kim was terribly upset, but Auntie soothed her disappointment by promising to take her to watch the wedding from across the street, along with Carole and Chris whom Auntie had agreed to look after for the day as a one-off.

I might have got the coveted bridesmaid's role, but I was still an inferior being when it came to the wedding arrangements. Nanny treated me with disdain, making it clear that she preferred the other bridesmaids – assorted Ponting cousins – and that I was there as a favour and had to do as I was told and shut up. Dad was the black sheep of the family and it rubbed off on us kids, no matter what we did or how hard we tried. And I did try. I was in awe of everything that was going on and could not believe I was allowed to be part of it, so I behaved as perfectly as I knew how.

Not long before the wedding I was sent on a holiday for underprivileged children: a week in a holiday camp, organised by the well-meaning NSPCC inspector, who persuaded Mum and Dad that it would do me good. Kim was to go too, but on a different holiday, after I came back. I was not sure about going, but then no one asked me. What I thought was of no interest to anyone. My biggest worry was that I had nothing presentable to wear. But luckily I was despatched to Auntie's for a couple of weeks before the holiday, and she made sure I had some nice clothes, which she packed carefully for me in a little suitcase. And of course I had no idea where I was going or what would happen – no one bothered to tell me.

On the day the holiday started I was very nervous, but Auntie put me on a coach already packed with other children and off we went. I sat next to a little girl called Sandra, who was small for her age. She was friendly and we whiled away the journey chatting. Sandra pointed out her brother, who was fifteen, sitting at the front of the coach. When we got to the camp we were shown to our chalets and told to get ready for the evening meal. I was sharing a room with Sandra, which I was pleased about, and the two of us unpacked together and washed our hands and faces before going over to the dining hall. The food was nice, and after tea a show was put on for us. By the time we got back to our chalet I was sleepy. Sandra, however, seemed agitated.

We said goodnight and went to bed, and I was asleep in seconds. But a while later I awoke to hear strange sounds. Peeping out from under my blankets, I could make out the outline of someone on top of Sandra in her bed. Horrified, I realised that someone was molesting her. I kept quiet, certain that I would be next. But after a few minutes the man got up, did up his clothes and crept out of the room. Not before I recognised him, though – it was Sandra's older brother. She was crying quietly in her bed. I reached out my hand tentatively towards her. 'It happens to me too,' I told her.

Sandra's brother came back to assault her most nights of our holiday, so although lots of fun things were laid on for us it was ruined for her and for me. We both spent our days dreading the nights. But, equally, I think we each found a little comfort in knowing that we were not the only ones. I felt terribly sorry for Sandra, but knowing that these awful things happened in other families made me feel a little less alone. At the end of the holiday we travelled back together and said goodbye when Auntie met me off the coach. We promised to keep in touch – but of course we did not. It was tough enough just surviving, and there was no room or time for anything else.

The wedding was due to take place two weeks after I came back from my holiday. On the day, all the bridesmaids were to get ready at Nanny and Grandad's house. A couple of them were the daughters of Bernard, Dad's middle brother and the only nice one. He took after Grandad, whereas Dad and Dave took after their haughty and distant mother. Bernard, a jolly man, called me 'Blondie' and always had a kind word. His younger daughter was friendly, but all the other bridesmaids looked down on me, no doubt taking their cue from Nanny. They were rude and unkind girls. I remember that one of them, back-combing my hair into a typical sixties' beehive, really hurt me, but when I cried out she just told me to shut it and complained that I had horrible hair that would not do what it was supposed to do. She squirted on so much hairspray that my hair felt like cardboard.

Still, when I was ready I glowed with happiness. A pretty kid who scrubbed up well, I felt beautiful and could not wait for the moment I followed Mary down the aisle. Left alone in the bedroom and told to wait until I was called, I danced around the room, imagining I was a fairy, pointing my feet in their little white socks and ballet shoes. At that point Dad came in. My heart started to beat madly and I knew what was going to happen. 'God help me' I pleaded to myself. Dad pushed me on to the bed, warned me not to make a sound and lifted my dress and petticoats over my head. Then I heard the door open and hopefully, I prayed that someone else had come in who would save me. My heart sank when I heard a man's voice say, 'My, she's a pretty one.'

Dad told the other man to get started and said he would watch the door. I heard him as he came towards me but could not see anything because of the lace of my voluminous underskirts. Then, with the same rough fingers as Dad, he started to tug the crotch of my knickers to one side. My hair was messed up and I could feel hot tears falling on to my rouged cheeks. I must have let out a sob, because he told me to shut up. Petrified, I could hear him undoing his flies and I could feel that I was leaking urine.

Then suddenly Dad was hissing that Nanny was on her way up the stairs and, after I heard the door open and close as the other man left hastily, he pulled me roughly off the bed on to my feet. Nanny was in the room surveying the scene. It would not have been hard to guess what was going on, confronted by the sight of a sobbing, dishevelled little girl. But Nanny simply said harshly to me, 'You get tidy and sort out your hair – you're a disgrace.'

If she had punched me it could not have hurt more. I realised that to her I was nothing, just a disposable child she had no feeling for. With my heart still pounding and my cheeks burning I tried to tidy myself up. But for me the wedding was ruined. I went through the ceremony in a daze, barely taking anything in and not caring at all how I looked. I just wanted it all to be over.

10

Independence

In September 1967 I started at Haggerston Secondary Modern School for girls. On my first day I
arrived feeling nervous and excited and lined up in
the playground with all the other new girls, waiting
to be told which class I was in. I was in awe of the
building, which seemed so huge and new. The
school was built on two storeys and divided into
houses, each with its own assembly room. Looking
at it from the outside, I wondered how on earth I
was going to find my way around.

I looked immaculate. The state had provided my
uniform: two sets of skirt, blouse, tie and cardigan,
plus one blazer and hat, all in a dull shade of grey.
Auntie had made sure I was scrubbed shiny clean
and that my shoes were polished until they
gleamed. The uniform, though hardly flattering,
made me feel very grown up; I thought the hat
made me look like an air-hostess. That did not last
long, though – on the first day I quickly realised
that if you wore it you got laughed at by the older
girls, and needless to say I never wore it again.

Among the sea of new faces I recognised one or two from my primary school. Miriam Ridsdale, 'Skinny Minnie', was there and so was Mary-Ann Merton, the stuck-up girl I had saved from choking. I would like to have been in the same form as Miriam, but we were sent off into different class-rooms. The girls were divided into six streams, and I was in the top one with twenty-four others. Our teacher was Miss Day, and our first job was to copy our timetable from the blackboard before the bell rang for our first lesson. There were so many lessons, all in different places, that it seemed quite overwhelming after Burbage, but Miss Day told us we would soon get used to it and packed us off for our first class.

I loved all the different classes and rooms. I could not believe the art room, which was full of all kinds of wonderful paints, paper, brushes and inks. I was good at art – I suppose I had inherited a little talent from Dad – and I loved these classes. The science labs were amazing too, superbly equipped and ruled with a rod of iron by the head of science, Mr Hughes.

We were each assigned to one of the six school houses and mine was Carnegie, which meant I got two purple stripes on my tie and a purple line on the V-neck of my cardigans. Miriam was in Car-negie too, so although we were not in the same form we sometimes passed each other in the corridor as we were changing classes, or met at lunch. The meals were fantastic. They were served in your own house assembly room and there was a big choice. Gone were the days of gristly meat and soggy cabbage; we got salads, chips, meat pies and all kinds of nice things. The only bad part was the embarrassment of handing in my free school dinner ticket every day.

From the start I loved secondary school, in particular the feeling of independence it gave me. I felt I could be me, Jeanette Ponting, and no one at school need know anything about my horrible home or parents. I was so proud, walking home with my bag full of books. This school represented a new start, and suddenly life seemed full of possibilities. In the first couple of weeks I made friends with three other girls in my class – friendships which were to last right through my time at school and well beyond. They were a vital part of my teenage years and helped to shape the person I became and the paths I chose.

First was Sherri Bonnici, who became my best friend. Sherri was very petite, with huge almond-shaped eyes and an amazing head of dark curly hair that hung down her back. Straight short hair was the fashion then and so Sherri hated hers, but everyone else thought it was gorgeous. She was the oldest of four children of a single mum who lived in an old house in Dalston which was due to be demolished. It still had only an outside loo so, like me, Sherri knew what it was like to be poor and to feel different.

Angela Donaldson was the tomboy of our group, though she did not want to be and she tried hard to change her image. She was fair with twinkling blue eyes and was also petite, but stockier than Sherri. Angela was a great athlete, good at all sports and a great fighter who would protect our group at all costs. She lived in the London Fields area of Hackney with her parents and younger brother, and had a hard life because her mum was very ill with kidney problems. Angela's father was Scottish and very strict, and she would have to hurry home from school to look after her younger brother and get her father's tea ready for when he returned from work.

Janet Barwell was the second eldest of eight children. She lived at Clapton Pond, which was further away from school than the rest of us. Janet was tall and, like me, strongly built and powerful. She had dark brown hair, a small nose, large brown eyes, a wide smile and great teeth. Both Janet's parents worked, so although there were so many of them at home she always seemed to be the most affluent of the four of us, with nice new shoes and whiter-than-white socks. Janet was an accomplished liar, which meant she could start trouble but was always the last person to get into trouble herself.

The four of us were all bright, but we stood out because we were clowns too. We all made our mark within weeks of starting at the school, and we were drawn to one another because so many of the other top-stream girls were boring and studious. We were never bullies – we were not unkind or horrible to others – but just joked around and loved to be outrageous. Too outrageous sometimes – when Sherri told the needlework teacher she was not wearing any knickers she was suspended for a week.

From the start we looked out for one another. When the first PE lesson came around we each needed a towel and soap. My towel was filthy and stinking and I had a grubby little sliver of soap. There was a loud-mouthed girl who made sure everyone knew, and I felt so ashamed I wanted to die. Most of the girls laughed, but not Sherri – she just handed me her own towel.

It was not long before Sherri invited me home to meet her mum, Jackie, and her brother and sisters. Their house was warm and welcoming, they were all lovely and I felt instantly at home with them. Jackie was an amazing woman – so different from my own mum. She had started her family early and seemed incredibly young and trendy. Tall and slim, with long, dark hair and a deep, sexy voice, despite having very little money she always looked fabulous in her mini-skirts and boots. Jackie was a survivor, strong and tough, and she was unconventional; she cared nothing for what people thought about her raising four children single-handed. And she always put her children first.

Sherri's soon became my second home. Life was not easy for Jackie and her family, but she always found enough food to feed me too. She was not much of a cook, however, and as I had had to learn at home I used to help her with meals. We formed a great bond: she taught me a lot about life and men, and I could talk to her in a way that I never could with my own mother.

Sherri's grandparents were lovely too. She and I used to go round to her nan and grandad's in Whiston Road near Broadway Market on a Friday after school. They were Jewish, and her nan would feed us bagels and smoked salmon and viennas, which were a kind of kosher hot dog. Like Auntie, she was very old-fashioned and concerned for her granddaughter. She used to remark on my amazing appetite, my height and my voluptuous figure and say to Sherri, 'Why can't you be more like Jeanette?' Conversely, when I took Sherri round to Auntie's she would marvel over my friend's hair.

What I loved most about Sherri and her family was that they never judged me. Sherri knew what sort of life I had at home, but there were no snide remarks and no power games. We became inseparable and discovered being teenagers, boys and life together. When I stayed with her we would sit on her bed late into the night talking about our hopes and dreams. Years later I named my daughter Martine Kimberley Sherri, in recognition of her great and generous friendship.

Not long after starting at secondary school I made a resolution – I would never let Dad touch me again. No longer was I the little girl who was terrified of him. He still scared me, but I had learned to outwit him. The next time he tried to touch me I told him if he did I would run away and report him to the police. After a couple more attempts he stopped trying and left me alone. In some ways I could not believe it had been that easy to stop him. After all those years of wetting myself with fear, lying awake at night sick with terror and being subjected to his disgusting perversions, all it took in the end was a couple of threats. But then I was not a small child any more – by the time I was eleven I was five foot eight and ready to punch anyone who tried to hurt me, including Dad. And, like all bullies, he caved in as soon as someone stood up to him. What did he care? After all, he still had Kim and Carole.

I felt terrible about that. Kim was nine and had been suffering at his hands for years. And Carole was four – how long would it be before he started on her? But, bad as I felt about Kim and Carole, I was desperately relieved to be out of it. I knew there was nothing I could do for them. Kim and I were still very close, but she was left behind at primary school. I knew things would not really change for her until she could join me at Haggerston.

Nowadays I stood up to Dad more and more. When we were out playing he would shout, 'Get in here' when he wanted us, and I would shout back, 'Not yet.' That won me respect from the other kids, and soon I became one of the top dogs among the gang. There were no more chants of 'Smelly Pontings' because I would lay into anyone who tried it. And in any case Kim and I were old enough to be able to wash ourselves and tidy ourselves up, even if Carole and Chris still looked like little ragamuffins.

Dad did not like it when I answered back, but he became more cautious about hitting me after I grew big enough and bold enough to hit back. He still did it, but less often. Mostly we stayed away from each other, and I began to spend a lot less time at home. I was not away all week like Laurence, but I grabbed any chance of freedom which came my way. As often as I could I went to Auntie's, where she always gave me a loving welcome and I got to see Laurence. And when not at Auntie's I often stayed with Sherri. Jackie never asked any questions when I turned up, but just treated me like one of her own. Before long Sherri's family were rehoused on the Holly Street estate and soon after that Jackie met a new man, John, who moved in with them. He was a huge man with a scar down the side of his face and at first I found him scary. But he was also a good man who never looked at me in a strange way or did anything he should not. He clearly idolised Jackie and the kids, and I soon came to trust him in the same way I trusted the rest of Sherri's family.

I did not go to Angie's much because her mum was so ill. We girls would sometimes go and hang around in her area, but she was never able to have anyone to stay the night. Sometimes we went round to Janet's. Miss Shaw, the deputy head of Haggerston, lived in her street, which was bad news for our gang who were keen to avoid her at all costs. But Janet's house was great – chaotic but welcoming, it provided another refuge for me. I was amazed by its size: it had a great big kitchen which was equipped to cater for eight kids plus visitors and was always immaculate. There was a great big urn that provided hot water, as well as a massive kettle of the kind normally only found in canteens. I could not believe the size of the family's daily order from the milkman – a whole crate of milk and several loaves of bread. And I was astonished that her mum, who worked all day, always managed to produce a meal for ten or twelve people every evening.

Our gang of four soon discovered cigarettes and

took to smoking behind the bike sheds at break. We felt trendy and grown-up as we stood around in a little circle, sharing one fag between us and watching out for prefects and teachers. We would pool our money to buy a packet of five Park Drive, which tasted pretty disgusting but were at least cheap. If we were really strapped we would buy a single ciggie for threepence.

All these friends, with their lovely families and welcoming homes, helped to distance me from Mum and Dad. They only ever came to one parents' evening, soon after I started at the school, and I hated them being there. Dad made an embarrassing effort to show off to the teachers, while Mum looked drab and out of her depth. I looked at Sherri and her trendy mum and prayed they would not think badly of me and that nothing would change. I need not have worried: Jackie probably noticed and understood a lot more than I realised, and the Bonnici home continued to welcome me.

I did not work very hard at school, but I still did well in plenty of subjects. The English teacher, Mrs Wagner, was lovely. I loved English, and even though I fooled around I found it easy. I liked reading books, writing stories and joining in discussions. Mrs Wagner gave us a mock exam, and when she read out the results Virginia Jacobs, the brainbox of the class who always studied hard, had scored 96 per cent and I was next with 95 per cent.

The whole class gasped and Mrs Wagner said to me, 'Just think what you could achieve if you really studied.' It was the same in history, where my project on Hitler got me another top mark. Mrs Rackham, the history teacher, once spotted a packet of Guards cigarettes and some matches in my open bag. She binned them but she did not punish me, which was pretty good of her. Out of the classroom I loved swimming and was in the school team, but as the cigs took over I slowed down. I did not care, though – I was young and free and enjoying myself. I was good at netball, too, but I found it boring and soon started writing notes to excuse myself, signing my Mum's name.

In my first term at Haggerston I started my periods. I was still only eleven, but my figure was already well developed. Mum, of course, had never mentioned periods to me and I would have been totally in the dark if I had not heard the other girls at school talking. I did not bother to tell Mum, knowing she would be no help, and managed things on my own. I often lacked the money to buy sanitary towels, but soon learned that a sock stuffed with toilet paper would do instead. Those were the days when you wore an elastic belt and the sanitary towel was attached to it front and back with two little loops. It was a cumbersome business and we all hated it because it was so messy. The only good thing was that you could not do sports when you had a period, so I could always use it as my excuse when I did not want to bother with netball.

It was not just periods that were difficult to manage. I was desperate to be clean and presentable for school, and that meant finding ways to wash, dry and iron my clothes. We never had any washing powder at home, so I would buy some with the money I earned doing a paper round and then wash my uniform in the basin and hang it out. I would also use my earnings to buy odd bits of uniform I needed, like tights. I could only afford one pair at a time, so at night I used to wash them out for the next day and if they were not dry by the morning I would put them on wet and then rub them with a towel to try and finish them off.

Jan and Angie were early developers like me. We all had boobs and looked older than we were, which we loved. Poor Sherri, who was still tiny and flat-chested, felt really left out. She used to stuff her bra with tissue paper and swap her flat school shoes for high heels whenever she could. We all started experimenting with make-up together, trying on the pale pink lipsticks which were all the rage but made us look like we had heart disease. We thought we looked wonderful!

For months I never dared ask anyone over to the flat, because it was too filthy and I dreaded any of my friends meeting Dad. But I felt really upset that I

could not have my friends round for a sleepover
like most of the other girls. One day I decided to
take a chance, and asked Mum and Dad if I could
have a friend over for Friday night. They said yes,
so I asked Angie. I knew she could not have anyone
over to her house because her mum was so ill, and I
thought she might like a break. I spent days pre-
paring, cleaning my bedroom from top to bottom,
washing the sheets, the floor, the walls – everything. I tried to clean the rest of the flat too, though
most of it was too filthy for me to be able to make
much difference. I sold my school dinner tickets
that week to get some money and bought treats for
us: bars of chocolate and cola. I had it all planned
and I was so excited. We would sit in my room
swapping girl-talk and sharing the chocolate and
cola, and then on the Saturday morning we would
go to the market.

Everything went perfectly. Angie came home
with me on the Friday and Mum and Dad said
hello and left us to it. We spent most of the evening
in my room. Kim was at Auntie's and Carole went
to sleep early, so we had peace and quiet. That
night as we lay in our beds we talked about boys
and what it would be like to go on a date. I was so
happy – I had a friend over and at that moment life
felt great.

I should have known it was too good to last. At
dawn we woke to the sounds of screams from my

parents' bedroom. I froze. Surely, surely they could control themselves when I had a friend in the house? I peeped over at Angie and saw she was awake.

At that moment our bedroom door flew open and there was Mum, stark naked, screaming, 'Help me Jen.' Before I could move Dad appeared, also naked, and, grabbing Mum by the hair, dragged her back into their room where the screams continued. I was sick, disgusted, heartbroken and deeply ashamed. I hated Dad. He spoiled everything. I hated both of them for their cruel, selfish behaviour. I wanted to be swallowed up by the earth. Hot tears of shame burned my cheeks.

Angie had not said a word about what had happened, and when I muttered, 'Sorry, Angie' she just said, 'Come on, let's get out.' We got dressed hurriedly and slipped out of the flat to the market, where we spent a couple of hours before Angie went home. We never mentioned the scene at home again. I dreaded the girls at school finding out, but Angie, kind-hearted soul that she was, never said a word to anyone. I blessed her for it.

11

Teenage Rebel

The gang of four – Jan, Angie, Sherri and I – spent most of our free time hanging around together. We often had nothing much to do and very little money, but it mattered not. We used to go down to Liverpool Street Station and watch all the City workers making their way home. There was a recording booth where for sixpence you could make a record – the old vinyl type – and we would go in there and record daft messages, or take turns making faces in the passport photo booth next to the recording one. Liverpool Street turned out to be quite a good place to meet boys, so we hung out there a lot.

Not that we did anything more than chat and flirt with the boys we met. We all talked about boys, but none of us was ready to go any further than fluttering our eyelashes at them – me least of all. The other three would giggle about sex and wonder what it would be like and when they would have their first boyfriend. But for me it was very different. I wanted a boyfriend too, but I had very mixed feelings about sex. I knew there was more to it than the horrible things Dad had done to me, but I could not imagine it feeling nice or ever wanting to do it, even with someone I liked. When one of the girls said, 'Do you know what a hand job is?' I thought, 'Know what it is? I've been doing it since I was five', and that made me feel old and sad.

I never said anything to my friends. I wanted to be the same, to be part of the group, so I played along, pretending I was curious and looking forward to it just like they were. But inside I felt confused. I wanted boys to like me and find me attractive, but when a boy did show an interest in me I felt scared and part of me wanted to run away. Dad had ruined so much for me. How would I ever let a boy touch me without thinking of Dad's filthy, rough hands? How would it feel if a boy tried something that my Dad had forced me to do? Would all the feelings of nausea and terror come back? Or could I feel differently if it was with someone special?

I had already decided that I was going to wait for someone I really loved and wanted to be with for the whole of my life. I did not want anyone thinking I was loose or easy, and I knew that when I did make love with someone I wanted it to be really special. Despite all that Dad had done my virginity was still intact, and I was not going to give it up until the right person came along.

Auntie's influence helped me a lot. She had always talked about finding someone special, about self-respect and the importance of waiting until it felt right. She gave me the guidelines which Mum and Dad never had, and I was determined to stick to them. Most weeks I managed to stay at Auntie's several nights, which was wonderful. The only bad aspect of it was the guilt I felt at leaving Kim at home to fend off Dad and look after the little ones.

Laurence was studying hard, so he did not go out as much as I did. Most nights he and Auntie and I would eat together before he went off to his books and I went out to meet my friends or did my homework and then curled up in front of the telly with Auntie. I loved being with my friends, but snuggling up with Auntie was still what made me happiest, especially if Kim was there to share it. One day Kim and I went out with some money we had saved to buy Auntie a present. At Woolworth's on the Holloway Road we got her a wooden squirrel with red stones for eyes. Auntie loved it, and we felt really special when she told us that she would keep it among her most treasured possessions in the glass-fronted cabinet in her living room. I used to love looking into the cabinet to see it still there.

Auntie was growing older now, and getting tired more easily. Even so, she still kept to her exacting standards, getting up at five to clean the flat and prepare for the day. We would hear her going over the rugs with her Bex Bissell carpet sweeper and bustling about with her dusters and cloths, just as she always had. When we got up she would be in the kitchen wearing the blue overall she had always worn, her red hair neatly pinned up in its incredible bun, and our boiled eggs would be ready on the table as ever. But the little signs of change were there. She needed to sit down more often, and we noticed that her sprightly pace had slowed a little when we went out shopping. By evening she was often worn out and needed to sit with her feet up while we made her a cup of tea. But we were not worried – we still believed she would always be there for us.

I would have been happy never to go back to Monteagle Court again, but although I often managed to stay away for a few nights each week I had to go back there the rest of the time. Nothing at home had changed. The squalor, dirt and smell were just as bad. There was still no food in the kitchen cupboards or the mouldy little fridge. Dad still sat in front of the telly with his cigarettes. He still beat Mum up and he was as cruel to Carole and Chris as he had been to us older ones. He still lashed out at Kim and me too, but he could not always corner us any more and it was often easier for him to spit insults at us and then turn his attacks on the little ones.

Carole and Chris were growing up as neglected as Laurence, Kim and I had been. They were both very subdued, quiet children – no doubt the result of being constantly mistreated by Mum and Dad. I loved them and felt sorry for them, but I did not feel close to Carole and Chris the way I did to Laurence and Kim. The gap between us was just too big and I wanted to escape, not to come home and have to look after them. Kim had started skipping school a lot since I had left Burbage. She hated being there on her own, and often did not bother. The NSPCC inspector was still coming round and he would talk to her, trying to persuade her to go to school. A man from the school board also came to visit her, but neither he nor the NSPCC man managed to persuade Kim that school was a good idea.

One day Kim decided she had had enough of the bugs which crawled over the flat – the bedbugs, lice and numerous creepy-crawlies in the loo. Without telling Mum and Dad she called the council's pest control department and arranged for them to pay a visit. A few days later a white van arrived and two men in uniform came to the door. They had masks on and each of them carried a large cylinder with a long tube and a spray-head attached.

Kim had timed it perfectly. Dad had gone out early that morning for a social services interview and she knew he would be gone for most of the morning. Mum was easy to bypass – Kim told her what was happening and she did not put up much objection. The two men spent the morning working their way through the flat, spraying a foul-smelling liquid all over the furniture, skirting boards, floors and walls. No corner escaped their attentions – the mattresses were turned and squirted on both sides, and we were told that it would take the morning to dry them out.

The two men advised Mum to keep the place clean, but we knew that was a vain hope. When Dad arrived home and discovered what had happened he kicked up a terrible fuss, but we did not care. Kim was triumphant that she had pulled it off, and for a few brief weeks the flat was bug-free.

We were all at Monteagle Court when Laurence's lung collapsed. He was thirteen. Laurence hated going home and spent his time avoiding Dad when he was there. I have always felt that his fear of Dad and the loathing he felt for him might have contributed to his problem. Laurence had had a weak chest ever since his pneumonia as a baby, and now that neglect came back to haunt him. He could barely breathe and I sat with him, stroking his face and trying to hide my fear, while Kim ran to the phone box to call an ambulance.

Laurence was in the Queen Elizabeth Children's Hospital in the Hackney Road for two weeks. Auntie, Kim and I went to see him as often as we could. Mum visited a few times, but Dad did not bother. When my brother came out of hospital he was thinner than ever. We took him straight to Auntie's, and it took several weeks of her care and good food to build up his strength again.

Sadly, Laurence's lung never fully recovered and it put paid to his hopes of joining the Navy – he realised the damage would show up in the rigorous medical he would have to pass. He was heart-broken. Although he stayed on at the Nautical School he knew he would have to give up his dream and find something else to do with his life. I felt sorrow for him, and hatred for Dad – the result of yet another instance of his cruelty, for it was his refusal to let Mum bring the pram inside the houseboat they lived in then that had led to Laurence's pneumonia as a newborn baby.

For my own part, I was now going through the various rites of passage of the teenage years. On the nights I stayed over at Sherri's her mum would let us go out – as long as we were home by 9.30. We always were, and Jackie trusted us and did not much mind what we got up to in the meantime. We would dress up to the nines and make ourselves look years older than we really were. Even Sherri could add on a few years with heels, a stuffed bra, plenty of make-up including false eyelashes and lipstick, and a skirt turned over at the top to make it shorter. This was the era of Mary Quant mini-skirts, thick eyeliner and shimmery pale lipstick and we made the most of it, pooling our resources to afford the make-up and swapping clothes.

If we had the money we went to the pictures, but we were usually broke and so we went to pubs or to the Jewish youth club Sherri belonged to, where we would hang around chatting to boys and enjoying ourselves. One night we went to a pub in Tottenham called the Spread Eagle, where I tried my first alcoholic drink. I was still only twelve and I asked for a gin and orange – one of the few drinks I had heard of. I thought it sounded so sophisticated and I knocked it back, followed by another. I was soon roaring drunk and fell about giggling, pulling Sherri's false hairpiece off in the process. She had had a drink too and was in as merry a state as me, so she did not even notice. We managed to get ourselves home and to bed without her mum realising what we had done. But the next morning we both felt terrible, with thumping heads and dry mouths. I could not believe this was what people called fun – I felt so bad I vowed I would never drink again.

In March 1969 I turned thirteen. At home there was the usual horrible fruit cake and not much else, but the girls at school made it a lovely birthday for me – the first nice birthday I had ever had. They all gave me cards and Sherri bought me a silver lip gloss, Jan a pair of tights and Angie a packet of five Park Drive ciggies. What made it so special was that I knew how little money they had – what little we had we would gladly spend on each other. That night we went to a pub called the Bird's Cage in Tottenham. We had all saved a bit of money and we dressed up in all our finery and went out to have fun. It was a glitzy pub and there were girls dancing in cages round the bar. We danced together to Tamla Motown hits, mouthing the words to each other. By the end of the evening we had spent our bus fares home, so we cadged a lift off a lad with a car. As we piled into the back I asked for his watch which I then dangled out of the window, threatening to drop it if he took a wrong turn!

Twice a year the funfair came to town – a big event. Everyone went, and it was an opportunity to meet boys and have some fun away from my parents. By this time I had become adept at lying to get out of the house. I would tell Mum and Dad I was studying at Sherri's – it almost always worked. We would arrive at the fair as the sun went down and the lights were coming on. The noise was deafening, with the roar of the machinery and music and stallholders shouting at us to ''ave a go'. Sherri and I always headed straight for the rides. We would go for the Waltzer, and songs like the Harlem Shuffle would be blaring out. The young lads who operated the ride were dark and handsome and always on the lookout for young girls to take round the back of the ride for a kiss and a cuddle. We never went, but there were plenty who did.

Sometimes Janet and Angie came out with us, too. But when we were thirteen Angie's mum died and Angie stopped coming to school. We did not see her for months and we missed her. Then one day she was back, and we all carried on together just like before. Angie did not talk about her mum, and neither did we. It was how we did things, then.

In September 1969 Kim started at Haggerston. We were both so pleased that she had got in and we could go to school together again. Once again it was Auntie who kitted her out and made sure she started secondary school looking scrubbed and neat. Kim was in Carnegie House too, but although we often saw one another we were worlds apart at school. By the time she arrived I had quite a reputation for clowning around, so everyone expected Kim to be the same. But she was much quieter than me and she soon made her own group of friends and stuck with them, while I was busy with mine. I used to help her with homework sometimes. We were both rotten at maths and would struggle through it together. When he was around we got Laurence to help us – what baffled us was child's play to him.

When Sherri was busy or on holiday, or if I was not allowed to go over to her house, I hung around with nothing much to do and in due course made friends with a girl from another of our flats. A couple of years older than me, Stacey had been dealt a rough hand in life. Her frail beautiful mother had died after a long illness and her father, a long-distance lorry driver with one arm permanently tanned from hanging out of the cab window, was a big, tough man who ruled the house with an iron fist.

Stacey had an older brother and sister and a younger brother. Her elder sister already had a baby and, as the baby's father had scarpered, she was looking for a husband. I did not like her father much, but he cannot have been all bad because sometimes he would come to the door when Dad was attacking Mum and try to calm things down. And every now and then he would take Dad off with him in his lorry for the day, to get him out of Mum's way.

Stacey had not inherited any of her mother's good looks: she had buck teeth and a hook nose. But she did have a fabulous figure and she used it to attract boys. At the age of fourteen she had become pregnant, but her baby had been taken from her and given up for adoption as soon as it was born. Undaunted, Stacey carried on giving herself to any boy she met. In the absence of good looks, sex seemed to be her way of getting young men to take notice of her. Looking back, it is easy to see that she was probably desperate for attention and affection, and her promiscuity was simply a misguided way of trying to get them. I also wondered whether Stacey had been abused, though I never knew for certain. At the time all we knew was that Stacey was a 'bad girl'. So bad, in fact, that Mum, no paragon of virtue herself, banned me from seeing her and told me she was a bad influence. This only made me want to see Stacey more; I always enjoyed doing things my parents did not want me to do, as a way of getting back at them, so I sneaked off with her whenever I got the chance.

Stacey and I had a lot of fun together. By the time I was thirteen and she was fifteen she was working in an ink factory and had a lot more money than me. She bought us both outfits that were the height of fashion in these days – tiny hot pants and white plastic boots, the kind with stretch elastic legs that you pulled up once the shoe part was on. We would put them on and go out to the pub thinking we looked gorgeous – we certainly looked much older than we were.

To me those nights out were wonderful: it meant a lot to me to have friends and a social life for the first time. I could get away from home and be myself, and I loved it. I never let a boy do more than give me a goodnight peck on the cheek, but Stacey was less careful and a year after she had her first child she was pregnant again. Despite her protests, her father insisted that her second baby be taken away and given up for adoption too. Stacey's only comfort was in the fact that the baby went to the people who had adopted her first child, so her two children would be together.

But not all my socialising involved under-age drinking and evenings spent with sadly promiscuous older friends. As a sporty girl I was excited when I got the chance to take part in a charity walk over the bridges of London. It was an enormous event – our school was taking part along with many others, and Sherri and I were among a coachload of kids dropped off at the start point. The walk – over one Thames bridge, along to the next, over that one and so on – was about twenty miles long, and by the end we were exhausted. But we had enjoyed it and met loads of other kids, among them two boys who asked us out that night. I was under strict orders to go home afterwards, but I soon found a way round that. I went home and told Dad I had come in the top ten on the walk and had to go back for an award ceremony in the evening to get my certificate. Lapping up the reflected glory in it for him, Dad bought the story and let me go.

Sherri and I met the boys at Dalston Junction station, near her house. We had managed to sneak into the loo there and put on our make-up and high heels and, as ever, rolled our skirt waistbands over to make them as short as possible before teetering out to meet our suitors. However, it was hardly a red-hot evening. The four of us went to a Wimpy bar and had a milkshake. After a couple of hours Sherri and I had to go, so the boys offered to see us home. Sherri and one of them went off in one direction, while the other boy took the bus with me and then walked me to my road. I said goodbye there, and when he asked me on a date I said no. He was nice, but not my cup of tea.

I was still waiting for Mr Right, but in the meantime I was curious about what it would be like to kiss and cuddle a boy. My chance to find out was not long in coming. Sherri and I had been asked to an all-night party and we were longing to go. We hatched a plan: she would tell her mum she was staying with me at Auntie's, and I would tell Auntie I was staying with Sherri. They were both used to us staying over and quite happy about it, so off we went to the party, dressed to kill – or so we thought – and giggling happily.

At the party I met a good-looking boy who seemed really keen. We started kissing, and he got as far as feeling my chest and a fumbled attempt at getting his hand inside my knickers, but that was it. It was enough for me; I didn't particularly enjoy it, but it made me feel one of the gang, the same as the other girls. It was part of moving on from the horrors Dad had inflicted and deciding that I would not let him ruin my life.

The next day Sherri and I swapped notes – we

had a pact that we would always tell one another what had happened. We used to talk about a boy 'tittin' you up', which meant he had felt your tits over your jumper. I pretended I had liked it more than I actually had – but then perhaps Sherri was being over-enthusiastic too. Impressing one another was probably the best bit for both of us.

When I was not out with the girls I often used to babysit for the family in the next door flat, a lovely Irish family called the Kavanaghs. They all had raven hair and blue eyes and were very attractive. The mum, Nell, was trendy and always looked immaculate. She loved to go out and had a soft spot for me. I was a good babysitter – I always got their two daughters into bed and fast asleep for her, and she paid me well. Mick, the dad, hated our Dad and they had quite a few shouting matches when Dad was hitting Mum, but like all the others who tried to help Mum he soon got fed up and realised it was a thankless task. The Kavanaghs never seemed to hold it against us kids, though, and we were good friends.

We kids would hatch plans all the time for making money. Guy Fawkes provided a great opportunity and we were pretty inventive about it. One year Laurence and I came up with a brilliant plan. He dressed as a guy and sat motionless on the ground while I asked passers-by for a 'penny for the guy'. If they failed to give us anything Laurence

would suddenly jump up and scare the living day-
lights out of them. We made lots of money that
year!

I was a bit of an entrepreneur, too. I used to go
down to Brick Lane Market and find bargains that I
would sell on at school or to local kids at a higher
price. I was still doing all the jobs I had done for
years – laundrette, grocery runs and errands for
neighbours, plus a paper round which was exhausting. I had to cart my heavy bag of papers up a
couple of blocks of flats where the lifts were often
broken. After staggering up four floors I just threw
the papers on to the doormats and then ran back
out, because these places were so spooky in the
dark of an early winter's morning. On top of this I
saved any money I was given. Ever since I had
grown old enough to grab my own birthday cards,
Dad had had to give up his scam of nicking whatever was in them, so I now got the money the
Ponting grandparents, Uncle Walter and Aunt May
and Auntie's sister Ninny sent me.

Despite my attempts to appear grown up when I
was out with the girls, occasionally I was reminded
that we were all really still kids who could catch
childhood ailments. Carole was seven when she got
chicken-pox. Mum said not to worry, as we had all
had it when we were small. She was wrong, though,
because a few days later Chris got it and a couple of
days after that I started to feel really ill. At first I

felt too ill to care, but after the temperature went and the spots came out I was horrified. They were everywhere – even in my hair. No one looked after me: I was left to deal with it myself. I cleaned the sink in the bathroom and then soaked a piece of sheet in warm water and held it over the spots, which were stinging and itching. I got Kim to buy some Calamine lotion and then covered myself in it, like a big pink blancmange! The worst part was that Dr Perkins had told me to stay inside for ten days, with no visitors. I hated doing so, but I was so bored that I actually did some studying, which I suppose was a good thing!

I was still off school when Valentine's Day came. A neighbour knocked on the door and handed me a card which said 'Jenny' on it and nothing else. It was from the boy I had met on the walk. Because he did not know which number flat I lived in, he had just put it through one of the letterboxes and hoped it would reach me. I was over the moon at getting my first Valentine's card, even though I had not much liked the boy.

A couple of days later I went outside to chat to Stacey and some of the others. I was not allowed back to school yet, but I was desperate to get out of the flat and have some company. Just before I got ill I had bought myself some beautiful mint green underwear, a bra and knickers, with money I had been saving for weeks. I had always had to use old bras of Mum's, so having one of my own was special and I thought this set was gorgeous. I put them on for the first time that day and went out feeling very pleased with myself.

Playing out at the front of the flats was a little girl called Georgette Williams. She was round the same age as Chris, and her mum, Pam, was the one who had helped to deliver Carole. Georgette asked me to swing her round, so I picked her up under her arms and started to spin. Suddenly I felt a terrible shooting pain in the top of my left thigh and I fell, dropping Georgette, who shrieked, and landing on the concrete on my knee. I was in agony, unable to move. Pam and a couple of the other mums came rushing out, and Pam knocked at our door and told Kim to fetch Mum. Hearing the commotion Dad rushed out, ready to act the concerned father, while Kim ran to the phone box and called for an ambulance.

I was taken to casualty at St Leonard's. Mum came with me, I suppose because the injury was pretty serious. I wished she had not done so, though – she was unwashed, with dirty hair, and despite being in intense pain I was embarrassed. My knee had ballooned to three times its normal size and I was scared. I was lying on a bed in a cubicle, the curtains drawn around me, waiting for a doctor to come, when my period started. Perhaps it was the shock that brought it on, but my beautiful new knickers were ruined. I was more upset over those knickers than over my knee, which turned out to have been broken in several places. The shooting pain in my upper thigh had been the ligaments straining, so when I fell my knee had taken the full impact.

I was moved by ambulance to the Metropolitan Hospital, a mile or so away, where I was taken to an operating room and the excess fluid was drained from around my knee. My leg was bandaged and I was given crutches and sent home to rest for a week, after which I would need to go back to have the knee put in plaster. At home my broken knee was the talk of the flats. Dad, who had to be the centre of any drama, insisted my bed was brought downstairs to the front room. I did not really want to share the living room all day with Dad, but nor did I want any rows. There I lay, while Dad sat in his chair watching telly and smoking all over me. I hated every minute.

A week later my leg was put in plaster and I managed to hobble back to school on my crutches. My friends all signed the plaster, and I got someone to write 'Neil Diamond' all down one side in big letters – I loved him! I was still hobbling around when Janet broke one of the fire alarms and everyone had to make a dash for it. I had to hobble at high speed out of the building, behind everyone else. Janet thought it was hilarious, but needless to say I did not.

I was in plaster for ten long weeks and had to have it redone halfway through because the cast had got so battered. Once it was off, my leg was revealed to have withered to nothing and to be covered in marks where I had stuck a ruler down the plaster to scratch. It was, understandably, very weak and I was told I had to go to St Bartholomew's Hospital in the City for physiotherapy. It was a lengthy bus ride away and I had to go on my own, but I went to all the appointments because I wanted to get my leg better again. I was also told to spend as much time as I could riding a bike. I did not have one, but Laurence did. He had saved for a long time for his bike, so I had to plead with him to let me use it, but he agreed and within a few weeks my leg was strong again, although my knee never completely recovered.

When I got back to school after my knee injury I discovered that my friend Miriam, 'Skinny Minnie', had left. I had no idea where she had gone or why. I missed Miriam and waited for ages for her to come back, but she never did and there was no way to find out what had happened to her. It was years before we came across each other again.

One winter evening I was round at Sherri's, swapping hopes and dreams as usual, before heading back to Auntie's where I was staying as much of the time as possible. I set off around nine, by which time it was very dark and there was ice on the ground. However, I was well used to the walk and by cutting through the back streets I could reach Auntie's in fifteen minutes. I headed down Station Lane, a road that was usually deserted at night, and suddenly I froze. I could hear the crunch of footsteps on the ice behind me, and something about their measured tread immediately rang alarm bells in my head.

I glanced behind and saw the figure of a man. I was sure he was following me. I told myself not to be silly, but a minute later I heard him shout, 'Blondie, turn around' and I turned to see him unzipping his flies and exposing himself to me, pumping away at his penis with a sickly grin on his face. I turned back and carried on, speeding up and wishing I had not worn the high heels that gave me blisters and meant I could only teeter along, sliding on the ice. He was still following me, so I bent down, took my shoes off and started to run barefoot, with the shoes in one hand.

As I crossed the grass verge at the entrance to Auntie's block of flats I could hear him close behind me, pounding along in his heavy boots. Suddenly I slipped on the icy grass and fell. As I rolled over he loomed over me and I was shocked to see that my pursuer was not some dirty old man but a good-looking boy of about seventeen. He leered down at me and began to masturbate again. I slid along the grass and scrambled to my feet. I set off again, running towards the entrance to the flats and shouting at him to back off, but he continued to follow. I decided to change tactics and stand my ground. 'What's wrong with you? Why are you doing this?' I asked him. But he just looked at me and grinned.

I reached Auntie's door and screamed through the letterbox for her to open up. The boy was not far behind me, so I aimed one of my shoes at his exposed penis and managed a direct hit. He squealed in pain, turned and ran down the stairs. When Laurence opened the door I gasped out what had happened and he set off in pursuit, but too late. The boy had gone. Kim was staying at Auntie's too, and she told us that the same boy had followed her the evening before. She had said nothing because she had not wanted to upset Auntie. Laurence was horrified and told us he would catch the boy and that meanwhile we should only come home together.

Kim and I were not settling for that, though. We had taken enough abuse in our lives and we wanted to catch him, so we came up with our own plan: the following night we would go out of the flats at the same time, each in a different direction. If he followed one of us, that sister would whistle for the other. We did not tell Laurence or Auntie what we were going to do – they would only have worried or tried to stop us.

The following evening Kim and I offered to go and fetch Auntie a bottle of her favourite Red Barrel ale. We set off together and then split up. I took the route I had taken the evening before while Kim took the longer one, where there were more people. I waved Kim off along the well-lit main road and took to the back streets, my heart in my mouth. There was no sign of the boy, and I decided that he was not going to be around that evening so I headed back to Auntie's to find Kim. When I got to the flats I saw her running towards me, shaking. She told me the boy had suddenly appeared as she passed the first of the blocks of flats. He had approached her, but luckily a neighbour had spotted her too and come over to say hello. The boy had taken off again, but Kim was now convinced he was local.

We went back to Auntie's and told her and Laurence what had happened. Auntie decided it was time to call the police. Next morning she, Kim and I visited the police station, where we were asked to go round the area with them in a police car to try and track the boy down. With a piece of extraordinary luck we passed him hanging around the first block of flats and were able to point him out to the officers. Once they had taken us back to Auntie's they went back to arrest the boy. Later that evening a police officer called to let us know that he would not be bothering us again.

I felt good. There had been times in the past when I had felt I had 'Abuse me' tattooed on my forehead. I seemed to be a magnet for dirty old men – and now even young ones – and I had had enough of it. Kim and I were not going to be victims; we were not going to put up with abusers who thought they could get away with frightening or hurting us. We were going to be brave and strong and show them that the Ponting girls were no pushovers – on the contrary, we were a force to be reckoned with.

12

First Love

My fifteenth birthday, the age at which I could legally leave school, was fast approaching. My English teacher, Mrs Wagner, asked Mum and Dad to come and see her at the school. She told them that I was a bright girl with real prospects, and that if they allowed me to stay on at the school I would be able to pass some O-levels and possibly go on to A-levels and get a really good job.

But Dad would not even consider it. 'A load of crap' was the way he dismissed Mrs Wagner's efforts on my behalf. 'You're getting a job and that's final,' he snarled at me. The family benefits would be cut back when I reached fifteen, and Dad wanted me to earn money to replace what he would lose. He did not give a damn what I did, as long as I earned. I had dreamed of being an air-hostess, travelling the world and looking glamorous in my uniform, but without qualifications of any sort I knew that my dream would have to be abandoned.

And so a couple of weeks after my fifteenth

birthday I left school, with no qualifications and a heavy heart. Sherri, Jan and Angie were leaving too. All the families needed the money. The four of us left school in a flurry of flour and water, laughter and tears, goodbyes and promises to meet up again. We all had jobs lined up to go to and, despite my disappointment at not staying on, it felt exciting to be going out into the world beyond school.

Janet had got an apprenticeship in a local hairdresser, Angie was going to train as a cutter in the rag trade, and Sherri and I had got jobs as trainee assistants with Marks and Spencer's at the Angel Islington. Getting the job was quite a triumph. We had to go through two lots of interviews, and waiting to hear whether we had made it or not was nerve-racking. When I got the letter saying I had been accepted I was walking on air, and when Sherri got the same letter it was even better.

We started on the same day, and felt very important as we put on our crisp blue overalls. Sherri was put on the food counters, while I was sent to men's underwear. Just my luck – men's underwear was the last thing I wanted. I dreaded middle-aged men winking at me as they picked out their vests and underpants, or, even worse, asking me to measure their inside legs. I wished I could have gone on the food counters too, but I had to do as I was told.

It was exciting to be earning my own money, and

Marks were nice employers. The food in the canteen was delicious and the staff facilities were really good; they even had a hairdresser we could use in our lunch hour. Being handed my first wage packet was brilliant. I was tired by the end of the first week – the hours were much longer than school, and I was on my feet all day. But when I looked inside my little brown pay envelope in the cloakroom it all felt worth it. Inside was ten pounds and seven shillings, and I felt rich. I had to pay Dad three pounds for my keep, but I still had enough over to buy myself a dress I had had my eye on and to go out with the girls. I was really pleased with myself about that. I had been sure that Dad would demand far more, or even try to take the whole lot off me. To avoid this I lied to him about how much I was earning, pretending it was a lot less, and he had reluctantly agreed that I needed to keep some money for bus fares, lunches and so on.

It was two months before we were allowed to operate the tills and then we were given our keychains, with the till keys and our photo passes dangling from the end of them. We felt very grand walking around with the chains hanging at the side of our overalls. Auntie was delighted by my job and told everyone she knew that her Jinny was working in a shop as grand as Marks and Spencer's. She used to come to the store just to watch me. She did not talk to me because she did not want to get me into trouble – but she would hover around so that she could enjoy the sight of me tidying my counters and serving customers. If no one was about she would give me a little smile and a wave before slipping out of the shop again.

Now that I was earning I looked forward to being able to buy Auntie some treats. I planned to save some money each week so that I could take her on a couple of day trips in the summer and repay some of the generosity she had always shown us. I could not wait.

A couple of months after starting at Marks and Spencer's Stacey and I went out for the evening in our multi-checked hot pants and boots. It was a weekday evening and, with nowhere special to go, we decided to visit a pub in Old Street called the Crosby Head. We planned to go on later in the evening to another pub called the Glue Pot where they had a live band.

The Crosby Head's public bar had a large, semi-dark room with a pool table to one side and a few tables scattered about. There were only two lads in there, both sitting on bar stools. My eye was caught by one of them, who had shoulder-length straight dark hair and gold-rimmed glasses. When we went over to order our drinks he started chatting to me and asked if he could buy me a drink. I said yes and asked for the poshest one I could think of – a vodka and lime. The four of us sat down together and he introduced himself as John Falconer, a twenty-one-year-old trainee structural engineer. He was well dressed in black trousers, a black jacket and a white shirt and I was struck by his accent and polite manner, his blue eyes and lovely smile. I was bowled over.

I had no idea what a structural engineer was, but it sounded impressive. Afraid that he would not be interested if he knew how young I was, I told him I was seventeen. For the next few hours we just talked, the visit to the Glue Pot forgotten. At the end of the evening he asked to walk me home and I said he could.

Stacey had been chatting to his mate, who was a fireman, although they had not hit it off the way John and I had. Since John had asked to walk me home, to be polite his friend came too, walking Stacey home. At the end of my street I insisted on saying goodnight, as always. John drew me to one side and asked for my phone number. Blushing with embarrassment, I had to tell him we did not have a phone. So he gave me his numbers at work and at home and asked me to call him the next day. Upstairs I told Kim all about the gorgeous lad I had met. I really liked him and wanted to see him again, but was very nervous about phoning. He was obviously from a nice home; what would he think when he found out what kind of place I came from – not to mention the fact that I was only fifteen?

The next day Kim kept telling me to call him and I kept putting it off. What if he told me to get lost? But then, he *had* given me his numbers. But then again, maybe he was just being polite. After agonising for most of the day I went to the phone box. Kim came with me and we squeezed in, with her saying, 'Go on' and me standing looking at the phone with a knot in my stomach and the piece of paper with his number on it in my sweaty palm.

Eventually I did it. His mum answered the phone and called him, and when he picked up the receiver he said, 'I'm so glad you rang. Do you fancy coming out on Friday?' I was over the moon. That Friday John took me on my first real date. We went to a film and then sat in a pub and talked and held hands and kissed. Nothing special, but to me it was magic. John had a warmth about him which made me feel safe. I knew I had found a good person, and I could not believe my luck. At the end of the evening he walked me home and asked to see me again a couple of days later. I happily agreed.

John and I started to see each other whenever we could. We met two or three times a week, sometimes more. He would wait for me outside Marks when I finished work, or else we would meet somewhere close, but not too close, to home. We spent our evenings talking, laughing and falling in love.

After two or three weeks I still had not told John

how old I was, and I was feeling more and more anxious about it. I knew I had to tell him – but would it mean the end of our romance? I could not bear the thought that he might walk away. One evening I plucked up all my courage and told him the truth. John took a sip of his drink, smiled and said, 'Yeah, I guessed that.' I was bowled over with relief. He knew the truth and he still wanted me! But then I was already beginning to learn that John was not thrown by anything; he was so calm and steady that he took everything in his stride. The one thing I was sure would end our romance was Dad. I dreaded John finding out about him, let alone meeting him. I was very careful to say little and always kept John away from our flat, telling him that my dad was strict and it was best he did not call round to see me.

One night, a few weeks after I had started seeing him, I had arranged to meet John in a pub. I was about to leave the house when Dad ordered me not to go. It was just the sort of power trip he loved – spoiling something he knew was important to me. He had been beating Mum up again and her face was tear-stained and bruised, her glasses broken for the umpteenth time. Her crime this time was buttering his bread when he had wanted it unbuttered. I hated seeing her like that, but nothing I could do would help and I hated being around the two of them even more – I just wanted to get out of the flat. Dad thought differently, though. I begged him to let me go, but he refused and insisted that Kim and I play Monopoly with him. I thought about making a run for it, but I knew that would leave Kim or Mum and the younger children to take the brunt of his anger.

It was with a heavy heart that I sat down to the game. I was terrified that John would think I had stood him up and that I would never get the chance to explain. As the minutes ticked by and I knew John would be waiting I felt more and more upset. I could not bear the thought that John might think I had not cared, when in fact I cared so much. I begged Dad again to let me go, but he was in one of his most vicious moods. 'Worried about yer boyfriend, are ya? Well, fuck him!' he sneered.

A little later there was a knock on the door. Before Dad could stop me I answered, and there stood John. He walked into the flat smiling, shook Dad's hand and said, 'Monopoly – great. Can I join you?' Dad was so taken aback that he said yes, and John was clever enough to see instantly that he had to let Dad win. After the game was over John sat and chatted to Dad for almost an hour.

Dad was impressed that I had managed to snag a bloke with a good job and a posh accent. He behaved himself, and even agreed to let me go out with John the next night. I could hardly believe it. John had not even blinked at the state of the flat, and he had handled Dad brilliantly. Nothing seemed to faze him. After that he came round whenever he wanted, though Dad was not always as friendly as he had been the first time. There were times when the two of them argued, and John would grab my hand and pull me out of the flat, muttering, 'You just can't reason with him.'

John's family were very different. He was still living at home, and one Sunday he asked me over for lunch with his parents. They lived in a new townhouse in Haberdasher Street, only a few minutes' walk from us. I was very nervous, but they were welcoming and made a big effort to include me. John had an older sister who was married and came to lunch with her husband. His parents had also fostered three younger girls, one of them severely disabled. That Sunday we all sat down to lunch together while the family scrutinised me.

I could see from the start that John's father did not think I was good enough for his son. He was gruff and rather short with me, and I got the impression he felt he was going to have to put up with me. John's mother probably felt the same way, but she was kind and polite to me and I was grateful. After that I joined them for lunch every Sunday and before long I was spending nights at John's house, sharing a room on the top floor with two of the foster daughters. Sometimes I would sneak down to John's room in the night for a quick cuddle, but we never went any further than that. I had told John that I wanted to wait before making love, and he accepted my stand and never pushed me. We did plenty of kissing and cuddling, but that was it – I just did not feel ready for anything more.

Laurence had made his escape from home and I knew I was on my way towards freedom, but I worried about Carole, Chris and Kim, stuck with Mum and Dad all the time. The two little ones had no one to love them or look after them except me and Kim, and I was not around for much of the time. Kim was like a mother to them, but she was still only thirteen herself and there was only so much that she could do.

Carole was now eight and seemed a lonely little girl. She was plump and wore National Health glasses, so she was an easy target for other children. They called her 'Four-eyes' or 'Fatty Pinky Pig' whenever she went out to play. As a result she took to spending hours in the bedroom playing with imaginary friends, and stopped going out to play at all. She was quiet and withdrawn, and I wondered what would become of her.

Chris was our baby. We loved cuddling him, and all the neighbourhood mothers cooed over him because he was so good-looking. He had big brown eyes and an angelic smile and was always eager and willing to please, running errands for anyone who asked and helping the local milkman with his rounds. Dad did not like Chris at all. If he was not being punished he was simply being a pain in the backside, and Dad ignored him most of the time.

I vividly remember the day, when Chris was just seven, when he became ill. Kim and I knew very quickly that something was seriously wrong. Chris was vomiting non-stop – he could not keep anything down, not even water. He was flushed and very hot, and we could see he had a high fever. I cradled his frail little body in my arms while Kim ran backwards and forwards to the bathroom to wring out a cloth in cold water so that we could try to cool him down. We told Dad he needed to see a doctor, but Dad insisted he was just putting it on. We pleaded with Dad to get help, but he refused. Mum did nothing either. Realising we were getting nowhere, Kim and I picked Chris up and carried him to St Leonard's.

In casualty a nurse had one look at Chris and took him through immediately. The doctors diagnosed acute appendicitis and told us they needed to operate before his appendix burst. Kim and I had to run home to get Mum to sign the consent forms, and then run back to the hospital as fast as we could. Even when, breathless and in tears, we told Dad what was happening, he just brushed it off. Chris had his operation a few hours later. Kim and I took turns to stay with him for the next few days because Dad would not let Mum come to the hospital. When he was allowed home we nursed him until he was better, but Dad, typically, never went near him or said a word about it to him.

My own life, however, was on the up and up. About six weeks after we met, John took me home to the flat one evening and came in to have a goodnight kiss. We were standing in the passageway when he said, 'I've got something to tell you.' My heart sank. This is it, I thought, he's going to pack me in. I've just found someone really special and he's going to end it. I froze, waiting for the blow, but John dithered and could not get the words out. 'I've been thinking,' he said. 'I wondered . . .' The torment went on for several minutes. Finally he got there. 'Look, I want to look after you. I want you to marry me.'

I was speechless. All I could do was nod. This gorgeous bloke I was madly in love with wanted to marry me. For the first time in my life something truly wonderful had happened to me. I wanted to burst with joy. In that moment all the demons of the past seemed to dissolve. Someone loved me. Someone wanted me. That meant there had to be something good in me, and I could not be all bad after all. Life seemed full of hope and promise.

After we had kissed passionately and John had gone I went up and woke Kim. 'I'm engaged,' I whispered. 'John just asked me to marry him.' Kim, still half-asleep, was stunned. She thought

John was lovely and was truly pleased for me. 'Wow,' she said. 'Engaged! You're all grown up.' That night I lay in bed watching Carole and Kim sleeping, hugging myself with happiness. I had found someone truly special, and he thought I was special too! Knowing that made me feel I could do anything. Nothing mattered any more except John and our future – at last I began to believe that I would soon be free of all the misery and squalor of home.

John, Kim and I kept the engagement a secret for the next few months. I was still only fifteen and we decided not to tell our parents until I was sixteen. My friends all met John and liked him. By this time Sherri too had found her own special boyfriend, a mechanic called Patrick who had adored her from afar for years, watching her every day as she walked past the garage where he worked on her way to and from school. He never did more than say hello and smile at her, but when she reached fifteen he made his move and asked her out. Sherri fell for him and the two of them were soon inseparable and, like us, planning marriage and kids. We went out as a foursome sometimes, but inevitably we were each wrapped up in our own romance and I did not see Sherri as often as I used to. But we made up for it in the breaks at work, regaling each other with the details of our dates and our plans for the future.

Stacey liked John too and was happy for me, but we soon saw a lot less of one another because I was so wrapped up in him that I had very little time for anything else. So it was a shock when one day Stacey told me that she was pregnant for the third time. We went out together and talked about it, and she told me that this time she was determined to keep the baby. She was seventeen, old enough to look after it, and she was not going to let her dad or social services take it away from her. She told me how much she loved the baby's father, but he did not want to know and so she was going to have to manage alone.

Soon afterwards Stacey told her dad about the baby and, after a huge row, he gave in and agreed that she could keep it. Social services agreed to find her accommodation where she could live with the baby once it was born. Stacey was ecstatic. A few months later she had a little boy and moved into her own small flat with him. We stayed friends, and I used to go round to see her and her son. Stacey was a good mum and had got what she had always wanted, someone to love. Although our circumstances were very different, I knew how she must be feeling and shared her joy.

13

A Funeral

One evening, a few weeks after John and I got engaged, Laurence appeared at the flat looking worried. He took me to one side and said, 'Jen, I need you to come to Auntie's. Strange things are happening. She keeps rambling and behaving oddly, like peeling potatoes and then boiling the skins and throwing the potatoes away. Today I got home from school and she was still in her dressing gown, wandering around the kitchen. I just don't know what's up with her.'

I had seen little of Auntie over the previous few weeks because I had been so involved with John. I had taken him over to meet her, of course, and she thought he was wonderful. But I had stayed with her on only a few occasions and had not noticed any changes, apart from the fact that she seemed to be getting much more tired. She had taken to going to bed very early so that she could still manage her 5a.m. start. Now I was concerned. What on earth could be going on? Why would Auntie do such odd things? I got my bag and caught the bus back to Auntie's with Laurence.

She was as pleased to see me as she always had been and set about making me something to eat. But I could see that a change had taken place. She was muddled, and would suddenly talk about things which made no sense. That night, after Auntie had gone to bed, Laurence and I talked. We did not know what to make of Auntie's state. She seemed to be not ill, just confused. We decided to keep a close eye on her and hope that she would get better.

Two days later, however, Laurence arrived back at the flat in a terrible state. Shaking and tearful, he told us he had come home from school that day to find Auntie lying on the bedroom floor, her head in a pool of blood. The blood was drying, which meant she had probably hit her head getting out of bed and lain there unconscious for most of the day. Laurence had run to the nearest phone box and called an ambulance, and Auntie had been taken to the Royal Northern Hospital.

When Laurence, Kim and I reached the hospital we were directed to a big, circular ward which we walked slowly around, looking for Auntie's familiar face. We could not see her anywhere. Eventually we found a nurse, who directed us to her bed. We had passed it earlier without recognising the frail figure lying in it, her head heavily bandaged. We hurried to hug her and reassure her that we would take her home and look after her. We had been told that she had had eight stitches in the cut in her head and apart from that was uninjured. But as we sat beside her bed she talked to us strangely. She seemed to think she was in the film *The African Queen*, with Humphrey Bogart and Katharine Hepburn, and had leeches stuck all over her which she begged me to pull off. I told her there were none, but it only made her more agitated and insistent. 'Take them off, Jinny, please,' she begged, and in the end the only way to calm her was to pretend to pick the leeches from her body, one by one.

Laurence and I left Kim sitting with Auntie and went to find a doctor. 'Mrs Hinton has senile dementia,' he told us. We had no idea what that was, so he explained that in Auntie's brain tiny blood vessels kept bursting. This was why she was disorientated and rambling. He told us she could not be treated and would not get better, and that we should be prepared for her to get worse. Then he said that as she was taking up a bed in a surgical ward he would have to discharge her. No one suggested that we might consult social services or get help for Auntie from community nurses. We were too young to have any idea about these things, and were simply left to get on with it on our own.

We got Auntie up, dressed her and took her to catch the bus home. She was shaky and fragile, and the journey to the bus-stop was slow. On the bus she wet the seat. We explained to the conductor that our auntie was not well, and to our relief he told us not to worry and helped her get off. At snail's pace, with one of us on either side, we got her home. Auntie was a well-known figure in the area and a couple of people waved to us and said hello. Auntie stared at them as though they were strangers.

Back in the flat, we took her into the bedroom and gently put her nightdress on her. Painfully conscious of the need to preserve her dignity, and knowing how mortified she would be if we saw her naked, we slipped her clothes off underneath the nightdress. Kim brushed her long hair, and we made her a cup of tea in her favourite china cup and held it for her as she sipped it. We put a plastic bag under her sheet in case she wet herself and then we settled her back on the pillows, sang to her as she had once sung to us, and watched her drift into sleep.

That night the three of us talked. We were determined to look after Auntie ourselves for however long she needed us. Laurence and I did not tell Kim what the doctor had said. Kim worshipped Auntie and, as she was only thirteen, we felt it would be too hard for her to know that something was wrong in Auntie's brain from which she would not recover. So we let Kim think that Auntie's frail state was simply the result of her fall, and that she would get better.

The next day I went to work and handed in my resignation. Laurence was already living with Auntie, and Kim and I now moved in full-time. We told Mum and Dad what had happened and that we were going to look after Auntie, but they expressed no interest apart from an angry complaint from Dad about the loss of my earnings. Kim, who had never been keen on school, simply stopped going altogether, so the two of us were able to stay with Auntie all day while Laurence was at school. When he got home he joined us, taking his turn sitting by Auntie or fetching her tea. Kim and I told him not to neglect his studies, and he managed to fit in his homework around his share of the nursing. Auntie's collapse had taken place during the summer holidays and by now it was early in the autumn term. Laurence was due to take his A-levels the following summer and we wanted him to carry on and do well.

Auntie would flit in and out of awareness. Sometimes she would suddenly come to and recognise us all. She would look surprised and say, 'Why aren't you at work, Jinny?' or 'What are you doing here, Kim?' I would tell her I had the day off and Kim would say it was a school holiday. She would nod in acceptance and soon drift off to sleep again, only to wake once more in the state of loss and confusion which was becoming increasingly familiar to us. We did everything we could to remind her of how she used to be. We splashed her favourite lavender water on her and held her special china cup while she sipped her tea, hoping it would make her feel better.

One day Mum came to see her. I was afraid that she might decide now was the time to unburden herself about the past, or, even worse, to ask Auntie for money. I took her into the living room and hissed at her, 'Don't you dare say anything to upset her. Don't you talk about Dad or money or anything else.' She promised and we took her through to Auntie, where Mum sat by the bed and cried and said very little, before slipping out of the flat again to return to Dad.

Between us we kept the flat clean, cooked for Auntie – making her soups – and nursed her, taking turns to sit with her through the night. We were afraid that otherwise she would wake confused or frightened – she slipped in and out of consciousness often and we did not want her to try to get out of bed and have another accident.

We had to do everything for her, washing and changing her, getting her up to go to the bathroom, and cleaning her up when she wet the bed. We kept the mattress covered with plastic bags, and once a day we sat Auntie in the chair in the bedroom while we turned the mattress and made her bed. Sometimes when I was bathing or changing her I would thank heaven that she was not fully aware of what was happening. During those moments I would whisper, 'Please don't let her come to her senses', because I knew the shame she would feel at this loss of dignity. Modesty had always been important to her; in the past she had never allowed us more than a rare glimpse of her bra and slip as she dressed in the morning. Most days she had been immaculately dressed and made-up, with her hair neatly done, by the time we woke.

We gave her a little silver bell so that she could ring when she wanted us, and she loved that. One day she said to Kim, 'I'd love a bit of scampi.' Kim did not know what it was and came to ask me, but I had no idea either. In the end we asked a neighbour, who told us we could get some at the fish and chip shop. Kim set off, but a couple of hours later she arrived back weary and empty-handed. She had been to every fish and chip shop she could find, but none of them had any. She was bitterly disappointed at letting Auntie down.

One treat we could easily obtain for Auntie was a bottle of her favourite Double Diamond beer. John and I would go over to the pub for a quick drink – a pint of Double Diamond for him and a Babycham for me – and then take back a bottle for

Auntie. We would get her up for a little while to sit in her favourite armchair and watch the telly, with a little glass of beer to sip. In those moments, when she was at her most lucid and able to enjoy this small treat, we all hoped, irrational though it was, that a miracle might happen and the old Auntie would be with us again. But it was not to be, and the flashes of Auntie as she had once been became fewer and fewer.

The neighbours all heard about what had happened to Auntie and did their best to help. Several of them brought soup or other dishes and left them outside our door, and one kind woman allowed us the use of her washing machine. We had been washing all Auntie's soiled sheets by hand, so we were very grateful. John came over to the flat regularly and often spent the evenings with us. He understood what Auntie meant to me and that I needed to be with her, and he did whatever he could to support us, including helping to buy food when we were short of money and helping Laurence with his maths homework.

The only money we had was Auntie's small pension. Laurence had found her pension book and we tried to get Auntie to sign it, but she could not. So I found her signature on one of her papers and forged it. The man in the local post office knew Auntie, and when we explained what had happened to her he told us he would cash the pension for as long as we needed it. We managed on this, but it was tough going.

In the evenings, once we had settled Auntie and one of us was sitting with her, the others would go into the front room and play records on John's portable record-player, which he brought over. We only had two records – Don Maclean's 'American Pie' and America's 'Horse with No Name' – and we played them over and over again. 'American Pie' was our favourite. We had no idea what it was about, but we knew all the words and would sing along. We whiled many hours away with our two records, or playing endless games of cards. We could not sleep with Auntie any longer, she was just too sick, so now we all slept on the front room floor, making ourselves beds from whatever cushions and blankets we could find and curling up side by side like a row of beans.

Auntie had a neighbour called Connie who used to pass the time of day with her regularly and comment on how well turned-out we were as small children. Connie lived alone on the ground floor of Laycock Mansions, and soon after we brought Auntie home she knocked on the door and said she wanted to help us. We thought this small, dark, kind, efficient woman was a guardian angel sent to help us. Connie was in her fifties, her children had grown up and left, and we never knew what had happened to her husband. Quietly and with no fuss she rolled up her sleeves and took over some of Auntie's care. She would often look after her for a few hours during the day, giving us time to go out shopping or have a break.

By this time Auntie had been in bed for several weeks and she had developed bed sores. Connie got medication for them and she also got in touch with social services who provided a proper polythene sheet for the bed and incontinence pads, as well as special straws for Auntie to drink through. After this contact a community nurse began to make regular calls. None of us had any idea Auntie might be entitled to anything, or how to go about getting it if she was, and Connie was the adult we so badly needed to help us cope.

Auntie's two sisters, Mary and Ninny, knew what was happening but had not visited. They seemed happy to let us get on with caring for Auntie, and as there had never been much love lost between them and us we were glad they stayed away. Then one cold winter evening, several weeks after we had brought Auntie home from hospital, everything changed. Mary and Ninny arrived at the flat and announced that we were not capable of looking after Auntie any longer and she was to go into a hospital. We were shocked. Surely they could not just arrive and take Auntie away? We were happy looking after her and the thought of her being in a hospital, all alone, was awful. But the two of them were insistent. As minors we had no say in what was to happen to Auntie, and her sisters, who had always treated us as intruders in her life and an unwelcome burden on her, had no interest in listening to us. We were brushed aside and told that an ambulance would be calling for Auntie the next day.

That night the three of us sat, silent with misery, by Auntie's bed. In the morning Laurence kissed her goodbye before going to school, while Kim and I waited with Connie for the ambulance. Connie was disgusted at what was happening, but she had no more power to stop it than we did. When the ambulance arrived, as the two paramedics helped her out of the flat we heard Auntie's frightened voice calling out, 'Where am I going?' We felt distraught, but there was nothing we could do except stand on the balcony and watch her being driven away.

That same morning Mary, Ninny and her daughter Cathy arrived to clear Auntie's flat. They packed the possessions of a lifetime into bags and boxes with lightning speed, and within a few hours the flat was stripped down to the last lightbulb. Even the lino on the floor was rolled up and taken away. The flat was to be handed back to the council. Desperate for some little part of Auntie to keep, I asked whether I could have the eggcup Auntie had used for her shillings for the meter.

'No,' I was told. 'Your job is done.' With shocking speed our beloved Auntie had been despatched and her flat, the warm and welcoming home which had meant so much to us all our lives, was dismantled. It was a brutal end.

Laurence, with nowhere to live, contacted his old friend Alf. They had always stayed in touch, and now Alf was able to get Laurence a room in the private house where he was renting a room himself. My brother, relieved that he would not have to go near Dad, moved in the day he left Auntie's. Kim and I had no choice but to go back to Monteagle Court, though I was often able to stay at John's which made things much easier for me. Kim had no such luxury, but Connie had told her to stay in touch and promised to take her to see Auntie, and she was true to her word. Three times a week they went together to Winchmore Hill Hospital, where Auntie was accommodated in one of the geriatric wards.

I had to find another job as quickly as possible. After a couple of weeks a jeweller in Hatton Garden, M.H. Meyer, took me on as an assistant. The job was not exciting, but at least I was earning again. I was put in charge of the mother of pearl and paste jewellery, which involved laying out the jewellery trays, serving customers and packing up orders. I seemed to have a talent for organising the window displays too, so I was often asked to help with those, which I enjoyed. The owner, Mr Gold-berg, ran a very regimented operation – our tea and lunch breaks were timed to the minute. But most of the small staff were friendly and I soon settled in.

For a few weeks I could not bring myself to go and see Auntie – it was as if I was in denial. I kept telling myself she was at home, just like always, well and happy, and that I would pop in and see her soon. It was John who persuaded me to go to the hospital. Auntie looked even older and more frail than she had on the day she was taken away. Her long hair was by now completely grey and hung down her back uncombed. But that day she was lucid. She said, 'Jinny, it's you.' I put my arms around her and we clung to one another. 'I don't like the food here,' she confided. 'And look at her, showing all her business.' I looked around to see an old woman sitting in a chair nearby, her loose hospital gown awry and no underwear beneath it. Across the way another old woman was throw-ing her food around and another sat, her top half-naked, staring into space. I wondered what on earth Auntie was doing in a place like this.

'I want my wedding rings,' she told me. 'Mary's got them. She says it doesn't matter, but it *does* matter. I don't want to be Miss Hinton – I'm Mrs Hinton.' I promised I would get them back for her.

A few days later I went to see Mary, who stood at her door as stiff-backed as ever and gave me a cool welcome. I asked her to take Auntie's rings back, and she agreed that she would. When I went back to see Auntie the following week she was wearing the three precious rings her Sid had given her. She took them off and handed them to me. 'I want you to have these, Jinny – one for you, one for Laurence and one for Kim.' I told her there was no need to give them to me now, and that I wanted her to wear them while she was in the hospital. She tried to insist I take them, but I refused. If only I could have known then how near the end she was, and that this would be her last opportunity to give them to me.

Kim had taken a job helping with children's donkey rides on Hampstead Heath. All day Saturday and Sunday and during the holidays, as well as on the days she bunked off school, she walked the donkeys up and down the same small stretch as one small child after another wobbled about on their backs. The money she earned she saved to pay for her visits to Auntie and to buy treats for her. Kim, stronger and braver than I was, would sit on Auntie's bed and comb her hair for hours. I found it terribly hard to visit because I could not bear seeing Auntie's loss of dignity, her frailty and her confusion. Kim's love for Auntie blinded her to these things; my love for her made me painfully aware of them.

Kim had been to see Auntie a couple of days after

my last visit and told me that Auntie's hair had been cut short. We were deeply upset, knowing how much Auntie's hair had meant to her. I told Kim I did not want to see her like that – if she came to her senses and realised what they had done, she would be distraught.

The following week I was in the kitchen at Monteagle Court, ironing a pair of loons – the trendy bell-bottomed trousers every teenager was wearing at that time – when Kim arrived with the most beautiful bunch of flowers. She had saved up to buy them for Auntie and was going to visit her. She asked me to go too, and I said I would follow with John once Carole and Chris were in bed. Kim decided to go up to the phone box by the Geffrye Museum to check on Auntie first. We did not normally do so, but for some reason today Kim wanted to.

Ten minutes later she walked back in, and I knew from her stricken expression that Auntie was dead. She had died three days earlier, but no one had bothered to tell us. I went through to Mum and Dad in the living room and told them Auntie was dead. I started to cry, and Dad got up to put his arms round me. But I felt the twisted look of triumph on his face. 'Don't you dare touch me,' I said, pushing him off. I ran to the phone box to speak to John.

Kim was inconsolable. She threw the bunch of

flowers in the bin and sat at the kitchen table, ashen-faced. When John arrived we asked Kim to come out with us, but she refused. We tried again, but Kim was adamant she wanted to be left alone. John and I walked the streets for hours. He listened while I talked about Auntie, about her love for us, her kindness, her funny little habits, her songs, her sense of pride and her belief in us. 'She's not really gone,' I kept telling him. 'She's here. I can feel her.'

Auntie's funeral took place a couple of days later. Kim had phoned Ninny and got all the details. Ninny said they had not been able to contact us to let us know, but we knew they could simply not be bothered. I could not face the finality of the funeral, so Kim went with Mum and Connie. Kim insisted that Mum should go and argued with Dad, who did not want her to. Kim would not give in and in the end Dad ignored them, while Kim made sure Mum was clean and presentable and got her out of the flat.

I got up and went to work and pretended it was a normal day. As I walked up the street I saw Auntie getting on a bus, her red hair and blue overall quite distinct. Why are they going to her funeral? I thought. She's right there.

That evening Kim told me she had been ignored at the funeral. No one had spoken to her, and neither Mum nor we three were mentioned when the vicar summed up Auntie's life. And Auntie, whose dearest wish was to be buried next to her beloved Sid, had been given a cheap cremation and had her ashes scattered to the wind. There was no memorial, no plaque, no sign at all to remind the world of the warm, vibrant woman she had been.

I continued to stay in denial for a long time. I suppose it was my way of coping with something I just did not want to face. I used to say to myself, 'I must pop up to Auntie's this week' and I would picture her in her flat, bustling about, humming to herself and looking forward to seeing us when we arrived. It comforted me to imagine her the way she had always been – strong, dependable and loving, and always there for her three little angels.

14

Triumph

My sixteenth birthday came and went a couple of weeks before Auntie died. In the midst of all the worry over her I barely noticed that the magic figure had at last arrived. John and I told both families that we were engaged, and he bought me a tiny diamond engagement ring from a jeweller in Hoxton. Dad was uninterested, as always, and Mum just said, 'That's nice' when she saw the ring. John's mum congratulated us warmly and said all the right things, but privately she told her son she was afraid I would hurt him. His father felt I was too young, and I suspect they both hoped that it would never come to a wedding. But John and I were oblivious to everything. We dreamed of married life, but we knew we would have to wait a long time. John was still very junior at work and needed more qualifications before we could afford a place of our own. But we had each other, and that was all that mattered.

I had dreamed for so long of being sixteen and being free. I was old enough to leave home. But where was I to go? I was not earning enough for a flat of my own and, although I already spent regular nights at John's home, I could hardly move in there full-time. Auntie's death affected me deeply and for several weeks I was so lost in grief that I found it impossible to think about anything else. But one evening John and I talked things over and decided we would live together. We were already engaged, and finding a flat would be the next step in building our life together.

Our high spirits were soon dampened. Since John was still training he did not earn a lot more than me, and we could not find anywhere we could afford. Then one evening John announced that he had found us a place in Clissold Park, at the northern end of Islington. We set off to see it, full of hopes and plans, but as soon as we got there I began to have doubts. It was four flights up, in a dilapidated old house, and consisted of a couple of tiny attic rooms – a bedroom and a main room – with cooking facilities on the landing outside and a shared bathroom. The two rooms were damp and dingy, with peeling paper, a few broken pieces of furniture and shabby curtains across filthy windows.

John looked at me and I put a brave face on. 'We'll make it nice,' I said, and on the strength of that and our longing to be together we went ahead and took it. We moved in the following week, each of us with a couple of bags full of possessions. I did my best to clean the tiny flat and make it cheerful, but it was a thankless task. We needed to redecorate and buy new furniture, but could not afford to do so.

Life in our own home turned out to be miserable and exhausting. We both had long journeys to work, and by the time we got back in the evening we were too tired to do much work on the flat or cook on the miserable little cooker. After two weeks we admitted defeat and asked John's parents if we could move back in with them until we found somewhere else. They agreed, and it was a big relief to leave that depressing little attic for the last time and go back to the warmth and comfort of the Falconers' house.

A couple of weeks later I returned from work to find a message from Kim asking me to go home. On the ten-minute walk back to Monteagle Court I caught sight of myself in a shop window: a tall, slim, blonde girl with a bright smile and a bounce in her step. I was wearing a new skirt I felt great in and I was happy. I was out of Monteagle Court, I had John, I had a job and life was full of promise.

My balloon of optimism was soon pricked. The door was opened by Mum, who said, 'Yer father's been nicked.' I went straight through to the living room to find out what had happened from Kim, and the story she told me made my blood run cold.

She had been worried about Carole for some time. Dad had taken to keeping her off school, saying she was sick when she plainly was not. He always chose days when Mum was not around much, and Kim suspected the worst. She often stayed off school herself to look out for Carole, but Dad was clever and there were times when he managed to get our little sister on her own. From her own bitter experience, Kim was afraid he was abusing Carole as he had abused us. Carole was a quiet girl though, and wouldn't tell us anything. We could never be sure. Unlike Kim and me, who loathed Dad and did our best to avoid him, Carole seemed to want to be with him and even defended him when he behaved appallingly. Perhaps it was because, unlike us, Dad and Mum were all she had ever had.

Kim told me that the previous evening she had gone with Stacey for a drink at the local pub. Since I had met John, and started to be around a lot less, Stacey and Kim had become good friends and Kim often went out with her to get away from the flat. The pub was quiet and the girls decided to go dancing at the Empire Ballroom in Leicester Square. Geoff, the lighting engineer there, liked Kim and always let them in for free and bought them drinks, so it was a cheap night out.

Kim nipped home to change out of her jeans, and as soon as she opened the front door she felt something was wrong. Mum was out for the evening on one of her now regular escapes and Kim could hear the telly on, but the living room was empty. She started to go upstairs and at that moment Carole came out of our parents' room, flustered and crying. Behind her was Dad, tucking his shirt into his trousers.

Kim took Carole by the shoulders. 'Tell me what he's done to you!' she shouted. Then she turned to Dad and started pounding him with her fists, shouting, 'You bastard, you fucking bastard. How could you do it?' It was as though all Kim's fury and hurt and pain through the years erupted at that point. She jabbed a finger in Dad's face. 'You'll regret this,' she hissed, and turned and ran back down the stairs and out of the flat. Dad was protesting behind her, yelling, 'I didn't touch her, you fucking mare. I didn't touch her.'

Kim ran to Stacey's flat and together they went to the phone box and dialled 999. 'I think my dad's been abusing my nine-year-old sister,' Kim told them. The police had always come when we called them, even if they ignored us and let Dad fob them off once they got there. This time they took Kim seriously, they must have heard the note of desperation in her voice. They came and arrested Dad, who was bundled into a police car, protesting and swearing, and driven away. Mum was home by that time, but there was nothing she could do except watch.

After they had taken Dad, Kim began to shout at Mum. 'How could you? How could you let him do it to us all those years, and now Carole too?' Mum, ever the victim, just buried her face in her hands and sobbed. She had no answers.

Upstairs, Carole and Chris were bewildered. Kim settled them into bed, telling Carole that what Dad had done was wrong and the police would not let him do it again. Kim tried to reassure her. 'Everything's going to be better now,' she promised.

The next morning Kim and Carole were taken to the police station. Both had to be examined by a police-appointed doctor and both had to give statements, separately. Kim told me they were taken to a large private house where a formal but kind doctor examined each of them. She heard him dictating the results to a secretary. When it came to Carole she heard him say, 'Broken hymen, internal bruising. Sexual interference has taken place with this young girl very recently.'

Dad was remanded in custody until a trial date could be set. We were free of him, at least until then, and perhaps for a lot longer. I hugged Kim. She had been brilliant. At only fourteen she had taken control of the situation. I was so proud of her.

As soon as Dad was gone the atmosphere in Monteagle Court changed. Kim cleaned the place from top to bottom. She played music, bought food and washed the clothes and the children, and within days it started to feel like the home it had never been before. I went round as often as I could. In Dad's absence Carole and Chris settled into their school routine and became more outgoing, and Kim blossomed into a confident young woman. She often saw Geoff, the lighting engineer from the Empire Ballroom, though only as a friend. I am sure he would have liked something more, but Kim was not interested and he respected her decision. He looked out for her, buying her drinks, chatting to her and making sure she got home safely whenever she went up there.

Even Mum seemed happier. Much to our amazement, she went out and got herself a part-time cleaning job. We had to laugh – she had never cleaned anything in the flat in her life. But she liked her job, working for a disabled woman and her husband, and the extra money meant she could buy some things for herself for the first time. With Dad gone Mum brightened a little and began to take more interest in her clothes and hair. She dyed her greying hair, and got herself a couple of new outfits. Even her posture changed: she held her bowed shoulders back and stood a little straighter. We were amazed by the change.

One day Kim told me that Mum had a lover called Jimmy, the man she was cleaning for. He would come round to the flat regularly, and Kim reckoned he gave Mum money for sex, on top of the cleaning. This did not stop Mum visiting Dad in prison, though. She would slip out regularly with a carrier bag full of magazines, cigarettes, chocolate and other goodies for him. Kim stopped her one day in disgust. 'How can you go and see him, after what he's done to all of us?' Mum was embarrassed. 'He's having a difficult time. I'm just taking him a few things to help him out,' she muttered.

The neighbours heard what had happened, and quite a few of them rallied round with help and support. Most of them were as glad as we were to see the back of Dad and they offered to help out with the kids or run errands if Mum needed them. Not everyone was kind, though. One day the word 'unclean' was daubed on our door in black paint. We felt terrible. It was like being picked out as plague victims. We cleaned it off as fast as we could, but the hurt stayed.

Kim, Laurence and I all met regularly to discuss the situation. Laurence had not been near Monteagle Court for a long time, but now he began to visit and all three of us tried to persuade Mum to divorce Dad. We hoped that if Mum divorced Dad and then he was convicted of abuse we would all be shot of him. But would Mum agree? Laurence worked hard on her, and she agreed to see a solicitor. He made an appointment and took her, and to our delight she agreed to go ahead. The wheels were set in motion and it looked as though the divorce hearing would be close to the time of Dad's trial.

While all this was going on John was as supportive as ever. I dreaded telling his parents about Dad, but John told them and they never said anything to me. His mother seemed sympathetic, but his father hated the whole thing and would grumble at John about the 'mess' my family was involved in. John asked him to be more understanding, explaining that he loved me and that what would help us most was his father's acceptance. His father did try, after that, but it was not easy for him.

Sometimes John and I would go and stay for a night or two with his sister, Jill. She and her husband lived in Basildon in Essex, and when we were there she allowed John and me to share a bedroom. This was lovely – we were able to cuddle up together at night and feel like a real couple. We still had not had full sex. Every time we came close I froze – the legacy of Dad's abuse, which made it hard for me to allow someone, even sweet, kind John, that close to me. He never pushed me. Nor did he ever ask me whether Dad had done to me what he did to Carole, though I am sure he guessed. I was grateful for his patience and sensitivity, because it was the last thing I wanted to think or talk about.

The months passed and Dad's case was post-poned more than once. The police assured us they had a strong case and were confident that he would be put away. Kim had also told them about the abuse she had suffered, and so had I. We felt quietly confident.

I had not said a word about Dad's case at work. The last thing I wanted was anyone's pity or contempt. At work I was just Jenny, an ordinary girl like all the others, and I wanted it to stay that way. Then one morning five of us were having our tea break in the downstairs staff room when Lesley, one of the more senior sales girls, said loudly, 'Oh, look at this in the *Hackney Gazette*.' She started to read the article out loud. '"A local man from Hoxton Market has been charged with the sexual assault of his nine-year-old daughter. Ronald Ponting has been remanded in custody, awaiting trial, for a further week."'

As she read it a feeling of nausea swept over me, and my face turned a deep red. I struggled to stop my hand shaking, but I had no control over it and some of my tea spilled over my hand and on to the floor. I hardly felt the burning liquid.

'Ronald Ponting,' Lesley said, looking at me pointedly with a smug little smile. 'Isn't he your Dad?'

At that moment I hated her. I was not going to give her the satisfaction of humiliating me and just shrugged. 'No, I've no idea who he is,' I lied. They all knew I was lying, but no one said anything more.

I struggled through the morning until the lunch break and then went for a long walk. I had not realised that anything about the case would be in the paper. Now my cover was blown: they all knew I was the daughter of a man who was accused of abusing his youngest daughter. I could not face staying, knowing that they knew. I went back and handed in my notice. That night I cried in John's arms. Was there no escape from the legacy of Dad?

A week later Mum's divorce case was due to be heard. A neighbour looked after Carole and Chris while Kim, Laurence and I took Mum by bus to the Law Courts in the Strand, where we met her solicitor. We were all nervous – the three of us because we so desperately wanted her to go through with it and Mum because she was terrified of the court, the lawyers, the judge and all the officials she was having to face.

We prayed that Mum would have the courage to walk away from Dad and start her life again. We had worked hard to persuade her that it was the right decision and to show her that life could be so much better for her without Dad. So much had changed since he had been in prison – her home was clean, she was not being beaten up any more, there was more food on the table, she had a job that she liked and her own money. She was not yet forty, and there was so much that she could still do. Would she give all that up to go back to a man who had hurt and abused her for almost twenty years? Surely not.

Mum had promised us that she would go ahead with the divorce. She knew what he had done, and enough was enough. We had convinced her that she needed to do it to protect Carole and Chris, if not herself. The papers were signed, the lawyers briefed, the court convened. All she had to do was go in there and tell the judge the truth. The solicitor had wanted to act quickly and to take the case to court while Dad was still on remand. This meant that Mum had to have grounds for divorcing him, and the solicitor confirmed that cruelty was the best option. He told us that Dad would be present in court, but that this was a formality and as long as Mum told them about Dad's behaviour and confirmed that she wanted a divorce she would get it.

We all trooped into the court and sat behind Mum's solicitor. Dad was on the other side of the room, and from the moment she went in he never took his eyes off Mum. Dad was called to give evidence first. 'Yer'onor, me and Lilian frequently 'ad baths together,' he told the judge. Laurence, Kim and I gaped at him. He had barely taken a single bath in all the years we had known him. Yet here he was, doing his best to persuade the judge that he and Mum had a happy marital relationship until his arrest. And even then, he could tell the court that Mum visited him in prison, bringing him food, magazines and cigarettes.

But Dad was hardly convincing, so we were not too worried. The success of the case depended on Mum's testimony. When she was called she stepped nervously on to the stand and stood there, looking down at her hands, as the solicitor began asking her questions. Mum was silent. The solicitor tried again. More silence from her. Eventually she spoke. 'I don't want a divorce,' she said.

Hot tears filled my eyes. Why was she doing this? Surely she could not go back on it now? But that is exactly what she was doing. She refused to look at anyone, her hands trembled and she would say nothing more.

The judge looked irritated and called off the case. Dad had won. His hold over her was so powerful that just seeing him in the court was enough to terrorise her again. Or perhaps she was just too used to him and too afraid of change. We would never really know why she did it, and in the end it did not matter. Within minutes we were all ushered back outside.

Laurence, his face distraught, told Mum he would never again set foot in Monteagle Court if she took Dad back. Kim and I begged her to change her mind. But it was no good. Mum's face was set in stone. 'I ain't goin' through with it,' she said.

The three of us walked away, close to tears. Laurence told us he would keep in touch with Kim and me, but that he had meant what he said – he was never going back to the flat. I went back to John's to break the news to him. And Kim, who had tried so hard to make the flat into a proper home and help Mum start a new life, had no choice but to go home, knowing that Mum had just chosen Dad over her five children. This had been her one chance to put right all the hurts of the past, to say sorry for all those times when she had turned a blind eye, knowing what Dad was doing, to show us that she could be there for us. But in the end she failed to do it. She had betrayed us one last time.

Only a week after the divorce case Dad's case came to court. The police and the prosecution lawyers, who talked to us regularly while the case was being prepared, seemed optimistic – we were assured there was a strong case against Dad, supported by medical evidence. Kim and I had both been told we would have to give evidence, and although we were nervous we were keen to do so. This was our opportunity to tell the truth and to put Dad behind bars and out of our lives for the next few years. There was no chance of us doing what Mum did and changing our minds.

The case was heard at the Old Bailey. The building was enormous, and going up the front steps and into the huge, hushed reception hall, with its high ceilings and uniformed staff, was a daunting experience. Mum was there, but she had refused to testify. A wife did not have to give evidence against her husband in those days and Mum was far too afraid to stand up in court and tell them what Dad had done, especially now she had refused to divorce him. But no matter – the important thing was that Kim and I would testify and so would the doctor. As for Carole, she was too young to go into the witness box.

The case started promptly at 10a.m. As witnesses we were not allowed into the court until we were called, so we waited outside. After a short while Kim was called in. I squeezed her hand and she followed the clerk inside. A few minutes later she came back and told me that she had only been asked her name, address and age before they sent her out again. She had no idea why. Moments later the kindly policeman who was liaising with us came out to tell us that a recess had been called as the prosecution wanted to put certain matters to the judge. We had no idea what that could be about; we just had to wait.

It was not long before he was back to give us the news. We were to be dismissed. The court had decided that my evidence was irrelevant, as I was not living at home when the offence was committed. Kim was considered an unreliable witness; presumably the defence lawyer had argued that she hated Dad and could have made the story up. As for Carole's evidence, she was so young that her statement had to be backed by a witness, and without Kim there was no witness. And the doctor? Surely, we thought, they would listen to the doctor. But the defence had presented another medical expert who had testified that Carole's injuries could have been caused by riding a bike. In the face of that, our doctor's evidence was not enough.

The case had collapsed. Dad was found not guilty and released. And Mum? She turned to us and said, 'Yer father's coming home.'

There are no words to describe how hurt, angry and betrayed we felt. Time after time, over the years, we had tried to tell those in authority what was happening to us. Now, at last, it had seemed as though we were going to be listened to and Dad would be put away. We had dared to have real hope. But in the end that hope was cruelly denied. Kim and I were terrified that Dad was now free to do to Carole what we knew had been done to us, and that he would continue to use his wife and children as punch bags. We had tried and we had failed. There was nothing more we could do.

The three of us and John went to the pub and sat round a table, disconsolate and silent. What was there to say? Dad was probably already back at home, giving Mum a beating for even thinking of divorcing him. Carole would be churning inside, as we had done when we were her age, knowing that Dad would be coming up the stairs to her room again that night. Chris, at only six, would know that the fear and misery and beatings were back.

That night Kim came to stay at John's with us. We could not let her go home straightaway. But in the end she had to, for she was still only fourteen and could not legally leave home for another two years.

With Dad back home everything went back to the way it had been before and the time when he was on remand seemed like a dream. The flat was stinking and filthy again, he was beating Mum as often as ever, and Carole and Chris were the same sad little kids they had been before – absolutely nothing had changed except that Dad felt more invincible than ever. For Kim it was a nightmare living with Dad again. He was afraid of her because she had reported him so he did not dare hurt her or beat her up, but he was vicious and cruel to her, making her life as miserable as he could and making it clear that he was in charge again.

Kim had already stopped going to school – she had not been able to face the others there once Dad's case hit the papers. Since then she had spent her days hanging around the streets or with Stacey.

So John and I came up with a plan to give her a break. We would take Kim on a holiday. We had very little money, but John suggested we hire a boat on the Thames for a week. It was generous of him – I knew he would have preferred it to be just him and me, but he knew how much Kim needed it. Apart from the awful NSPCC efforts we had been sent on Kim and I had never had a holiday before, so we were both wild with excitement. We decided that John would be the captain, I would be the first mate and Kim the cabin boy. We spent our evenings planning what to take and I took Kim to the fashionable King's Road to buy her a pair of loon trousers and two T-shirts.

When the day of our holiday arrived we took the train to the boatyard where we were shown to a long, narrow canal boat, the *Celeste*. It was cramped but very neatly arranged, and we loved it. John and I were on the put-you-up bed in the main living room, while Kim had a bunk in a separate little room. There was also a tiny kitchen and bathroom. John was shown how to operate the boat and off we set, Kim and I giggling and heady with the newness and adventure of it all.

We spent the whole week laughing, and it re-stored Kim and me to normality after the awful shock of the two court cases. It was warm and sunny and we spent our time on deck, all mucking in together as we steered the boat through one lock after another, drifting gently down the Thames. John had to empty the chemical loo and he had hurt his ankle, so he had to hobble along carrying the bucket which Kim and I found hilarious. And Kim liked to impersonate Long John Silver, hopping along the boat with one leg behind her, saluting and calling John 'Cap'n'.

In the evening we would moor the boat and go off to a local pub for a couple of hours. One evening it started to rain, but we thought it was only a shower and when we got back from the pub we just went to bed. But in the early hours Kim woke John and me because she had felt the boat moving. We rushed out to find there had been so much rain that the river had risen – the boat had broken free of its moorings and was heading fast towards a large weir. We all yelled 'Rapids!' and leaped into action, managing to turn the boat and reach safety by a hair's breadth.

During that week away I began to feel truly free of Dad for the first time. He could never hurt me again, I knew that, and in John I had someone who could not have been more different – a kind, loving man who had already stood by me through so much. I trusted him totally. Although we had kissed and cuddled and spent nights in one another's arms when I had sneaked downstairs at his house or when we were at his sister's, we had still not made love. Now, floating down the Thames in our little canal boat heaven, I felt ready. We made love, and it was as tender and beautiful as I had hoped it would be. At the end of the week both Kim and I felt happier than we had in a long time. We both knew that we had the future to look forward to and good times ahead. Dad had not broken us, and he never would.

Once we were back in London I needed to get another job fast, and a few days later I managed to find a temporary job at an employment agency. While I was there I made friends with a young woman called Sue, and when she was offered a job as manageress of a branch of a leading employment consultant she asked if I wanted to come with her. I leaped at the chance of working as an assistant consultant, and from the moment I got there I loved it. My new office was in the West End, which meant an hour's journey each way, but I loved the buzz of the West End and I loved the job. I was dealing with customers, which I soon found I was good at. And the pay was better than anything I had had before. I was able to buy some smart clothes for work and felt like a real young woman about town.

My next problem was where to live. I could not stay at John's for ever, and the two of us still could not afford to get a decent place together, so I decided to look for a flatshare. Every day I trawled through the papers until I found something that sounded perfect, in a nice street in the middle of Islington not far from Chapel Market. When I went round there the landlord took me up to the first-floor landing. The flat had a large front room, a kitchen big enough to eat in and two bedrooms. I would be sharing the larger one with another girl, while a third girl was in the smaller one. The bathroom was up a stepladder in the attic. I loved it. The other girls were not home yet, but I said I would take it even before meeting them and told the landlord I would move straight in.

That evening I met the others, who were both older than me and both about to leave. Glyn was off to the Lebanon to teach English and Lyn, my room-mate, who came from Wiltshire, was feeling homesick and thinking of going home. Soon after Glyn left a girl called Jenny Wyman arrived. She was from Torquay in Devon and was dying to enjoy the bright lights of London. When Lyn left soon after that, Jenny's friend Sylvia arrived from Torquay to take her place. Sylvia and I hit it off instantly and knew we would be friends for life. We went shopping together, did our laundry together and went out in the evenings together when I was not seeing John.

Before she was fifteen Kim had met her first real boyfriend. His name was Graham and he was several years older than her, but he seemed as keen on her as she was on him. Graham had wild, curly hair and wore purple crushed velvet trousers with holes in the crutch and knees, tie-dyed orange T-shirts and open-toed sandals. He looked a bit like Mick Jagger and hung out with a bunch of friends who loved real ale, cricket and Jimi Hendrix. I was not mad about him myself, but I could see that Kim was and he made her happy, which was what mattered. She spent as much time as she could with Graham, staying with friends or with me. Kim was in love, and she knew she would soon be free of home and Dad and living her own life.

Laurence was making a success of his life, too. He had passed his A-levels and was training to be an accountant, he had a room in a nice house and he was still good friends with Alf, the man who had become a surrogate father to him.

And me? I had John's steady love to support me through anything, and with my new job, my new flat and my new friends I felt truly independent for the first time. Still not yet seventeen, I felt free of the past and ready for all the adventures that lay ahead. With the optimism of youth, I believed nothing would ever go wrong again. I was going to survive the nightmare of my childhood and was already feeling strong and confident and full of hope. I was me, Jenny Ponting, and I was on my way.

Postscript: Survivors

A few years ago Kim called and asked me what the best news I could hear would be. 'Winning the lottery,' I replied. 'No, better than that,' she said. 'The old man's dead.' We both screamed with delight and I can still see Alan, my husband, looking at me in disbelief. It suddenly dawned on me that even Alan, the man who knew me better than anyone else in the world, could not conceive of what this news meant to me. I felt free, I felt elated.

It was only after the euphoria had passed that I realised how sad it was that I felt this way. My father, the man responsible for my very existence, had died, and I could only feel relief. I wondered whether, before he went, he had felt even a moment of guilt or remorse. But I doubted it – that was not a road Ron Ponting ever went down. He died of a stroke brought on by severe diabetes. He was seventy-six and he and Mum had been married for almost forty-five years. The only one of his children who went to his funeral was Carole.

Mum and Dad had of late been living in a small warden-assisted retirement flat, where I had last visited them a few years earlier. Their new home was no more pleasant than their former one had been. It was filthy and grimy and Dad ruled from the armchair he was by then barely able to leave, while Mum pottered about trying to manage whatever needed to be done. Her eyesight had become very poor and she spent a lot of the time dropping things and then searching for them.

After Dad died I went to see Mum again one more time. It was her birthday and I took my son LJ, who was then eleven, and my husband Alan. Kim came too. Mum was not yet seventy, but seemed far older. She had had a triple heart bypass some years earlier and was in poor health. Her walls were covered in photographs of her children and grandchildren, religious pictures and rosary beads. Around her were piles of videos. Beside her on the table was a picture of Dad – a frail, sickly, sallow old man, propped up in a chair asleep. Mum looked at it fondly and talked about how much she missed him and what a wonderful life they had had together. Listening to her was difficult. I wanted to shake her by her frail shoulders and say, 'How can you not remember?' I couldn't wait to leave. Mum told us she was planning to go and live with Carole and her family, and I wished her luck. I left feeling frustrated and resigned. Mum would never change: she had already reinvented the past, and perhaps that was how she coped. I could not help a moment of sadness too, though. She had never been a real mother to me, and a little part of me, deep down, still wished that it had been different. But when I walked out of her door that last time I let that part go. I had needed a mum when I was little. I did not need one any more.

Over the years it was friends who helped me survive and stood by me – I could not have made it without them. I am still in touch with some of my closest friends from the past. Sherri is always there and, although we do not speak that often, we do catch up from time to time. No matter how much time goes by, she is still the same fiery girl she always was and still a wonderful friend. Sherri had a period of bad health, but she survived and has a son and is happy living in Bury St Edmunds in Norfolk.

Angela became a community worker. She had three sons and is now a grandmother. Janet married a hairdresser and lives in Edgware with her husband and two sons. It is nice to know that we all made it. Stacey is another friend who stayed in touch over the years. After keeping her son she went on to marry and have a daughter. For a while we lived in the same block of flats and our daughters played together as youngsters. We had a good friendship for many years. We still exchange Christmas cards and she has a good life.

Not long ago I decided to visit the Friends Reunited website and look up my old school. Suddenly there was a blast from the past – Skinny Minnie! I sent her an email and soon afterwards we spoke on the phone, delighted to find one another again. After she vanished from school all those years ago I never knew what happened to her, so it was wonderful to catch up. She told me that way back then her mum died and she, Skinny Minnie, was left to care for her family. Eventually she was taken into care, which she says saved her. She now lives happily in Canada with her husband and two daughters, and I hope to visit her there one day. We have shared many memories on the phone, and she has helped me remember so many little things that I had long forgotten. Thanks, Miriam.

I have never forgotten John, my first love and the man who showed me, after so much disillusion and hurt, that men could be loving, kind and sensitive. I thought I would be with him for ever, but in fact we parted when I was eighteen. Too young to settle down and too hungry for life's adventures, I needed to explore and grow. But I shall always think of John with warmth for his generosity and support. I look back on our time together with the happiest memories. John helped me to turn from an abused, scruffy little girl into a self-assured young woman with confidence and belief in herself. I sometimes wonder which way my life might have gone without John.

At eighteen I believed, as young people do, that I was invincible. I thought that all my mistakes were made and all the pain was behind me. But I was to discover, in my next relationship, that it was not so simple. The legacy of my childhood led me to another difficult, abusive man, and it took me several years to break free and to realise that I was worth more. The blessing in that relationship was my beautiful, talented and loving daughter Martine, born when I was just twenty. Martine has brought me so much happiness. I am enormously proud of her, not just for her acting and singing success and her sparkling beauty, but for the person she is – a warm, generous and loving daughter. Having Martine to care for and fight for saw me through the darkest times, as I struggled to help her father and eventually realised it was impossible and parted from him.

When Martine was just five years old there was a tragedy which changed our lives. It was the summer of 1981 and my sister Carole was visiting. We were close then – Carole was eighteen and she often called round to see Martine and me. It was very hot, all the windows were open and the summer breezes wafted through my basement flat. Martine's father had been arrested on assault charges and remanded in custody and, painful as it was, I was relieved that he had been locked away and could not hurt us any more.

Chris, our baby brother who was then seventeen, had babysat for Martine two days earlier when I had gone to court for the case. Afterwards he met me at a local pub to hand Martine back. Chris often babysat: Martine adored him and he liked to come round to my flat, glad to escape, as all of us had been, from Monteagle Court. He had become a beautiful young man, fragile, funny, lovable, sensitive and caring – just the kind of qualities which enraged Dad. But everyone else loved Chris because he was so charming, good-natured and eager to please.

That day, as Carole and I chatted, the phone rang. It was Dad. 'You'd better get down here fast. Your brother's dead,' he said. Minutes later we were at Monteagle Court. Laurence was already there – the first time he had returned since he swore to Mum outside the divorce courts, nine years earlier, that he never would. He and I went with Mum to the friend's flat in which Chris was staying a couple of streets away. The door was open and the police were there. Chris lay wrapped in a foetal position on an old scruffy sofa, a glue bag over his face. Our beautiful angel was dead.

It took a long time to get over Chris's death. Dad never appeared to suffer, but for the rest of us it left a huge hole in our lives that has never been filled. It marked the beginning of change in all of us. Mum returned to her Catholic roots and went to confession more and more. Kim's marriage to her first love, Graham, came to an end, and I felt the need to get away and begin again. Laurence went to Chris's funeral and then walked away again, never to return.

Kim was the one I stayed close to. We had shared so much for so long that the bond between us was unbreakable. I have always had enormous respect for the way she coped when she was the one left behind. Kim walked out of Monteagle Court when she was fifteen and pregnant. She married Graham when she was sixteen and had a beautiful daughter, Carrine, and later a son, Daniel, both wonderful children. She is a grandmother now, and loving it. After training as a psychiatric nurse she had a long and successful career in mental health nursing before joining the police force and ending up as a senior manager. Kim's life has not always been easy, but I have the greatest admiration for her. With her big heart and great sense of humour she is an ally, a friend, a sharer of memories, hopes and dreams, and a wonderful sister.

Laurence, determined and ambitious, went on to become a very successful and wealthy businessman. He married three times and had a child, and for many years we stayed close. A few years back we grew apart when our lives went in different directions, but I will always have a place in my heart for the brother who fought so hard and with such courage to protect us when he was just a skinny little kid.

As for Carole, we remained close for many years. She was a troubled soul and I did my best to help, but in the end our differences were too great. Carole always stayed closest to Mum and Dad and was always the first to defend Dad. It was as though she never really saw him for what he was. I found that hard, but perhaps it was her way of getting through. Like Kim and me, Carole married early. She had six children before her husband died and she became a young widow faced with the tough job of bringing up her children alone.

None of us had an easy time with relationships. After I broke up with Martinc's father I went through a couple more tough relationships and then found happiness with John McCutcheon. This marriage was blessed with our lovely son LJ. Sometimes things just don't turn out the way we wish, but after a divorce and some time on my own I met my soulmate and second husband Alan, a warm, loving man whom I feel very lucky to have found.

Despite turbulent times, I have always been a survivor. Life went on to throw all kinds of adventures, hardships and tests at me – all of which are another story – but somehow I came through. At the hardest moments I have always remembered what Auntie used to say: 'No matter what happens, hold your head high, put on a smile and be the best you can be.'

My great blessing has been my two children, my son LJ, now thirteen and growing up into a lovely, thoughtful young man, and Martine. Seeing her grow into the stunning young woman she is today has been a joy. Martine has always been there, no matter what, and the two of us are very close. She never misses an opportunity to spoil me and has given me some of the best gifts, holidays and parties ever. A while ago she threw a party at the smart West End hotel Claridge's for my forty-seventh birthday. I arrived thinking I was there for a family dinner, but when the doors opened I was stunned and delighted to see many friends, old and new. It was a marvellous evening, and there were times when I had to pinch myself to believe my marvellous good fortune.

As I sat at the top table with my wonderful daughter, my husband, sister and close friends, I thought how proud Auntie would have been and how happy Chris would have been for me. They never lived to see the person I became, but I know they were there with me in spirit that night. As I glanced round the tables at all the smiling faces I

felt true warmth and love. It took me a long time
and a lot of heartache to learn that we should never
carry the shame and guilt of others. But I have
finally got there, and now I feel truly free.

Barnardo's

GIVING CHILDREN BACK THEIR FUTURE

Barnardo's works with 120,000 children, young people and their families in more than 361 projects across the UK. This includes work with children affected by some of today's most urgent issues: poverty, homelessness, disability, bereavement and abuse.

Barndardo's vision is that the lives of children and young people should be free from poverty, abuse and discrimination and its purpose is to give the UK's most vulnerable children and young people a better start in life.

Barnardo's are pioneers in providing help for sexually exploited children and young people, investing in more community services in this field of work than any other children's charity. The 16 UK-wide services based within local communities provide children and young people aged between 10 and 18 with a safe place to go for practical help, advice and emotional support and help in changing their lifestyle.

For more information about Barnardo's, visit our website at www.barnardos.org.uk